WHERE IN THE WORLD IS THE PHILIPPINES?

WHERE IN THE WORLD IS THE PHILIPPINES?

Debating Its National Territory

Rodolfo C. Severino

Carlos P. Romulo Foundation

Philippines

ISEAS

INSTITUTE OF SOUTHEAST ASIAN STUDIES

Singapore

First published in Singapore in 2011 by
ISEAS Publishing
Institute of Southeast Asian Studies
30 Heng Mui Keng Terrace
Pasir Panjang
Singapore 119614

E-mail: publish@iseas.edu.sg
Website: <http://bookshop.iseas.edu.sg>

Co-published with
Carlos P. Romulo Foundation
30th floor, Citibank Tower
8741 Paseo de Roxas
Makati City, Philippines
<www.carlospromulo.org>

The responsibility for facts and opinions in this publication rests exclusively with the author and his interpretations do not necessarily reflect the views or the policy of the publishers or their supporters.

ISEAS Library Cataloguing-in-Publication Data

Severino, Rodolfo C.
   Where in the world is the Philippines? : debating its national territory.
   1.   Jurisdiction, Territorial—Philippines.
   2.   Territory, National—Philippines.
   3.   Territorial waters—Philippines.
   4.   Philippines—Claims to Sabah.
   5.   Philippines—Claims to South China Sea.
   I.   Title.
KPM2055 S49   2011

ISBN 978-981-4311-70-0 (soft cover)
ISBN 978-981-4311-71-7 (hard cover)
ISBN 978-981-4311-72-4 (e-book PDF)

Typeset by Superskill Graphics Pte Ltd
Printed in Singapore by Utopia Press Pte Ltd

CONTENTS

Foreword   vii
Professor Dr Hasjim Djalal

Carlos P. Romulo and the CPR Foundation   xi

1.   Introduction   1

2.   The Colonial Legacy   5
     The Coming of Spain   6
     The 1898 Spain-U.S. Peace Treaty   6
     Mindanao and Sulu   10
     Batanes   18
     The Maritime Jurisdiction   19
     The 1935 Philippine Constitution   20
     The Debate Continues   22

3.   The Territory of an Independent Nation   26
     The 1973 Philippine Constitution   26
     The Baselines and the Sabah Claim   29
     The 1987 Constitution   31
     The Question of Internal Waters   33
     Decisions Must be Made   35

4.   The Claim to Sabah   39
     British Moves and Philippine Arguments   40

The Creation of Malaysia and the Philippine Response   44
Jabidah and the Baselines Amendment   51
Dropping the Philippine Claim?   54
Normalizing Philippines-Malaysia Relations   58
Pressing the Philippine Claim   60
Conclusions   61

5.   The South China Sea   66
     The Cloma Claim   67
     The Philippine Claim   69
     China's Claim   74
     Vietnam's Claim   78
     Malaysia and Brunei Darussalam   80
     UNCLOS as Watershed   82
     Dealing with China   84
     The Declaration on the Conduct of Parties   88
     The U.S. Involvement   93
     The Possibility of Resolution   95
     The Informal Workshops   98
     Conclusion   99

6.   Philippine Maritime Jurisdiction and UNCLOS   105
     UNCLOS   107
     Philippine "Reservations"   108
     Decisions Required   112
     Overlapping EEZs   114

7.   What Next?   121

Index   125

About the Author   132

FOREWORD

The Philippines was, and in my mind still is, an ardent supporter of the development of the concept of archipelagic states in the Law of the Sea. The Philippines, together with Indonesia, Fiji, and Mauritius, participated actively in the first meeting of the archipelagic states in New York on 13 March 1972, working together to formulate the principles for the archipelagic states, including their rights and obligations, to be submitted to the coming third UN Law of the Sea Conference, which was to start in 1973. They were able to agree tentatively on four principles, although they still had some basic differences on the details, especially on the criteria for their status as archipelagic states, their rights and obligations over the archipelagic waters, and the rights of other states over those waters. At the suggestion of the Philippines, another meeting was held in Manila on 25–26 May 1972 (Mauritius did not participate in the Manila meeting), attempting to further formulate the agreed principles. After lengthy discussions, including on a trip to Corregidor across Manila Bay, three basic principles were agreed on – the definition of an archipelagic state, the sovereignty of an archipelagic state over the waters within its archipelagic baselines, and "innocent passage" of foreign vessels through such sealanes as may be designated by the archipelagic state.

These three principles were later introduced during the third UN Law of the Sea Conference, which began in New York in 1973 and lasted until December 1982 in Montego Bay, Jamaica. The UNCLOS 1982 incorporated these basic principles after their development, "amendment", and regulation into nine Articles (Articles 46–54).

Many years after the Law of the Sea Conference, I engaged Rodolfo C. Severino in discussions on Law of the Sea issues. There is no doubt that he understands the basic elements of the Law of the Sea Convention, particularly the Philippine position on some of the major issues.

One of the most perplexing issues was the nature of the lines drawn by the Treaty of Paris of 1898, in which Spain delivered sovereignty over the Philippines to the United States. The Philippines later claimed that the lines were "territorial" in nature and encompassed an expanse of sea outside of the Philippines island group, up to the extent of some 250 miles from the Philippines' coast lines. In fact, those 1898 lines also included an island that was part of the Dutch East Indies, later recognized as such in the Max Huber Arbitration in 1928. (The island is now part of the Indonesian archipelagic state and one of Indonesia's outermost islands.) Many observers consider the 1898 lines as basically "allocation lines", indicating that the islands within those lines were transferred by Spain to the United States, not "territorial lines", since Spain did not have "sovereignty" over the extensive seas beyond the Philippine Islands at that time, and therefore could not have transferred what it did not have.

Both Indonesia and the Philippines originally considered the waters inside the Philippine baselines as "internal waters", but recognizing "innocent passage" through those waters. After ratifying the 1982 UNCLOS, Indonesia basically adopted the UNCLOS provisions, and therefore recognized the principle of "archipelagic waters" with the rights of "archipelagic sealanes passage" through certain designated "archipelagic sealanes" in the archipelagic waters. Beyond the archipelagic sealanes, Indonesia also recognized the right of "innocent passage" for foreign vessels, except through "internal waters" inside the "archipelagic waters" as stipulated in Article 50 of UNCLOS. The Philippines, however, for a long time regarded the waters inside the baselines of the archipelagic state as "internal waters", and therefore was not able to determine the archipelagic sealanes as stipulated in the UNCLOS 1982, as Indonesia has already done.

If the Philippines still considers the 1898 lines as territorial, thus the limits of its territorial sea, it would of course be interesting to ask from where the Philippines would measure its Contiguous Zone, Exclusive Economic Zone, and Continental Shelf, because these three UNCLOS regimes would be considered *beyond* the territorial sea (Article 33, Article 55, and Article 76(1)).

Like other archipelagic countries, the extent and scope of the Philippines' national territory depend on the maritime regimes that it adopts for seas around the archipelago and between the islands.

The Philippines is among the few nations that define their territories in their constitutions. Those definitions mostly antedate UNCLOS and, therefore, could clash with the Convention's provisions.

The Philippines is a party to UNCLOS, which prescribes, in rather precise ways, the maritime regimes for signatory states.

Severino traces the historical evolution of the constitutional provisions on national territory and, just as importantly, the Philippines' attempts to expand its territory by asserting claims to territory beyond the Treaty of Paris limits, on which the original Philippine territorial concept, dating back to colonial times, was based. Later claims include those to land features in the South China Sea and to Sabah.

One effect of the uncertain nature of the Treaty of Paris and of the claim to Sabah: the excruciating pace of negotiations to delimit the maritime boundary between Indonesia and the Philippines where their maritime regimes overlap. Thus, Indonesia cannot complete the definition of the extent of the waters around its archipelago, especially the Contiguous Zone, the Exclusive Economic Zone, and the Continental Shelf bordering with the Philippines, although some progress has lately been achieved after decades of negotiations.

At the same time, Severino cites instances of recent Philippines Government attempts to reconcile maritime claims with UNCLOS provisions. Foremost among these is the 2009 legislation declaring regimes of islands for the land features in the Spratlys that the Philippines claims. To be sure, the legislation, as he points out, does not designate which are islands and which are mere rocks, "which cannot sustain human habitation or economic life of their own (and, therefore,) shall have no exclusive economic zone or continental shelf." (UNCLOS, Article 121(3))

Severino does not for the most part prescribe solutions to settle whatever inconsistencies may exist between the Philippines maritime claims and UNCLOS provisions, to which Manila is committed. The most that he does, for example, is to nudge the Philippines' policy more closely towards UNCLOS and urge that China (and Chinese Taipei) and, subsequently, Vietnam scale down their own claims to vast expanses of the South China Sea, claims which many believe cannot hold up under UNCLOS.

Instead, he seeks to shed light on issues involved in each important case and urges the Philippines Government to resolve them wherever possible and as quickly as possible. He cites likely consequences of not doing so, including poaching in claimed Philippine waters by foreign fishing vessels with impunity and the inability of law-enforcement agencies to enforce Philippine laws in those waters.

Meanwhile, the workshop series on managing potential conflict in SCS continues among relevant ASEAN authorities and China/Chinese Taipei.

Severino acknowledges little prospect for the settlement of conflicting territorial claims anytime soon or successfully negotiating some overlapping maritime regimes, although the recent Malaysia-Brunei agreement is a step in the right direction. But he points to increasingly better prospects for managing disputes and keeping them from erupting into violence and, therefore, for keeping the area peaceful, stable and mostly free for navigation and overflight, provided states abide by their commitments and rhetorical promises.

It is for these reasons that Rodolfo C. Severino's book on the Philippines' national territory is of utmost significance for all international lawyers, particularly those who pay special attention to the development of the Law of the Sea. In particular, it would be a significant contribution to clarifying at least some of the ambiguities in the Philippine positions and could also be an encouragement for the Philippines' authorities to seek solutions to those questions, including those that Severino raises in the book.

Professor Dr Hasjim Djalal, MA
Member of the National Indonesian Maritime Council,
former Vice Chairman of the Indonesian delegation to the
Third UN Law of the Sea Conference

Carlos P. Romulo and the CPR Foundation

Carlos P. Romulo was a Filipino soldier, journalist, diplomat, author and educator who devoted his life to global peace and security. A basic truth that General Romulo expressed throughout his life, again and again, is that peace can be achieved only when there is economic security. "Peace is impossible without freedom," he said before the Philippine Chamber of Commerce in February 1948. "Freedom, in turn, is impossible without economic security."

Established in 1996, the Carlos P. Romulo Foundation was inspired by the memory of the General and of his dream of living in a secure and peaceful world. It is an independent Philippine organization that helps define the roles the public and private sectors play in the pursuit of peace and prosperity. Committed to promoting peace and development in the Philippines and the Asia-Pacific region, the Carlos P. Romulo Foundation is a private non-profit think-tank that brings together scholars and decision-makers from different parts of the world to discuss public policy and its impact on peace and development.

Its inaugural activity, a conference entitled "Deepening Asia-Pacific Cooperation", brought together twenty representatives of government, academia and the private sector from eleven countries to discuss political/security cooperation, economic cooperation, and private-sector participation in the Asia-Pacific region. Roberto R. Romulo, son of General Romulo and Chairman of the Foundation, co-chaired the conference with Han Sung Joo, director of the Ilmin Institute of International Relations, Korea University.

General Romulo was a staunch advocate of international cooperation and the free market. As early as 1945 he foresaw that the Pacific, and not the Atlantic, would be the wave of the future. When socialism and central planning were the rage in 1955, he believed that the market, and not the state, would propel the region to record growth and development. A firm believer in interstate cooperation based on sovereign equality, Romulo devoted all his energies to this vision in his more than fifty years of public service under eight Philippine presidents.

In today's global environment, where governments are no longer the sole power-wielders, collaboration between the state and the private sector has become increasingly essential. As the private sector's clout continues to grow, so does its potential to contribute to world peace, freedom and human development. The Foundation provides neutral forums for bridging government, academe and the private sector, with the goal of harnessing this potential.

The Foundation also serves as an objective source of reliable analyses, to which Philippine political leaders can turn for sound policy guidance and from which corporations can glean insights about the opportunities emerging in the Asia-Pacific region. At the same time, it provides opportunities for scholars to dialogue with business and government decision-makers and get a practical look at public policy.

In 1998 the Foundation organized "Philippine-American Relations in a New Century". Among the American speakers were former U.S. ambassadors to the Philippines: Stephen Bosworth, Michael Armacost, Thomas Hubbard and Nicholas Platt. Filipino speakers included ASEAN Secretary-General Rodolfo Severino, Secretary of Foreign Affairs Domingo Siazon, and Secretary of Trade and Industry Manuel Roxas II. Key speakers from the business community included Maurice T. Greenberg (former American International Group chief) and Jaime Augusto Zobel de Ayala (Chairman and CEO of the Ayala Corporation).

As part of its efforts to bring international affairs to the top of the national agenda, the Foundation organized a debate among the country's top presidential candidates during the campaign period of the 2010 national elections. Presidential candidates Senator Richard Gordon, National Defense Secretary Gilberto Teodoro and Senator Manuel Villar gamely expounded on issues, such as achieving peace in the Philippine South, combating terrorism, growing foreign trade and investments in the country, establishing policies and improving conditions for Filipino labourers abroad, and boosting the Philippines' international competitiveness.

With Philippine President Benigno Aquino III taking the helm in 2010, Foundation activities in the years following his election will support efforts aimed at redefining the nation's place in the emergent global and regional order. Linkages with other institutions, such as the Johns Hopkins School for Advanced International Studies, will be actively pursued, and joint activities brought to fruition. The Foundation will also conduct studies and undertake seminars designed to develop Philippine thought-leadership on relevant issues; for example, ASEAN community building, refining the Asia-Pacific political/security architecture, sustainable economic growth, and information and communications technology.

This "re-engagement" initiative reaffirms the Foundation's role as an intellectually rigorous institution dedicated to providing new perspectives to enhance the Philippines' global competitiveness. Moreover, it is a response to President Aquino's call to action and appeal for reform. For, as General Romulo said in a speech at the United Nations Appeal for Children in 1948, "Peace does not depend on the actuations of nations but principally on the actions of individuals. If we must insure the peace of the future, all precautions should be taken now."

General Romulo's career as a public servant included seventeen years as Secretary of Foreign Affairs and ten years as the Philippines' ambassador to the United States. In World War II he was aide-de-camp to General Douglas MacArthur. He became a brigadier general in the U.S. Army, receiving the Purple Heart and the Silver Star for his service during the War, and later a major general in the Philippine Army.

As a journalist he wrote a series of articles, after a tour of what was then called the Far East, about Japanese imperialism, and predicted an attack on the United States. For this he won the Pulitzer Prize in Journalism for Distinguished Correspondence. He also authored twenty-two books, three plays, and several poems. In 1982 he was named a National Artist for Literature by the Philippine government. He was conferred the first Bayani ng Republika Award for his outstanding service to the Filipino nation and the rank of Raja of the Order of Sikatuna, an honor usually reserved for heads of state.

Referred to by his colleagues as "Mr United Nations", he was elected president of the United Nations General Assembly in 1949 — the first Asian to hold the position — and served as president of the UN Security Council four times, in 1981, in 1980 and twice in 1957. As a signatory of the charter forming the United Nations in 1945, he spoke the famous line, "Let us make this floor the last battlefield", at the first General Assembly.

By the time he died in 1985, one month shy of his 88th birthday, he had served on the boards of a number of prestigious Philippine corporations, such as San Miguel and Equitable Bank. "The General," as he was widely known, had received well over a hundred awards and decorations from other nations as well as over sixty honorary degrees from universities all over the world. Extolled by *Asiaweek* as "A Man of His Century," he was the most admired Filipino in international diplomacy in the 20th century.

To learn more about the life of General Romulo, log on to www.carlospromulo.org.

Carlos P. Romulo Foundation

1

INTRODUCTION

Where in the world is the Philippines? In other words, where does the Philippines have jurisdiction? Of what kind? Where does that jurisdiction end? Because the Philippines is an archipelago, that is, a nation of many islands, these questions apply importantly to the country's maritime regime. In contemporary terms, what is the extent of the Philippines' territorial sea? Its exclusive economic zone (EEZ)? Its contiguous zone? Its continental shelf? From where does or should the Philippines measure its territorial sea, contiguous zone and exclusive economic zone? What is the character of the large expanses of sea between some islands of the Philippines? What is the nature of the Philippine claim to the Kalayaan Island Group? What about the Philippine claim to Sabah?

For most countries, questions similar to these and the answers to them are fairly straightforward. They have long been settled, and other countries have accepted, or at least acknowledged, those answers. However, in the Philippine case, many of the questions remain unanswered. Fierce, often arcane debates go on within the government, in the academic community, and, of course, with other, especially neighbouring, countries. Once in a while, the controversies erupt into public view. One example is the case of the agreement between the Philippine National Oil Company and the China National Offshore Oil Corporation on a Joint Marine Seismic Undertaking and the subsequent agreement among these two firms and their Vietnamese counterpart to convert it to a tripartite endeavour. Another is the new legislation on the baselines from which to measure the territorial sea, the contiguous zone, the extended continental shelf, and the exclusive economic zone. In a move to make the country's declared maritime jurisdiction compatible with the 1982 United Nations Convention on the Law of the Sea (UNCLOS), the new baselines

law declares a "regime of islands" with respect to Scarborough Shoal and to
the land features in the part of the South China Sea that the Philippines
claims. Enactment of the law immediately elicited protests from China and
Vietnam, both of which claim all of the Spratlys, as well as disagreement, for
other reasons, from some Philippine academics and legislators. China also
claims Scarborough Shoal, which it calls Huangyan.

The result of all this uncertainty, which the Philippine Government is
now attempting to reduce, is that Philippine law enforcement agencies have
not been sure of what to allow and what to prohibit where, particularly by
way of sea passage, overflight, fishing activities, and environmental protection.
The protection of the resources in the purported Philippine EEZ has been
uncertain, inconsistent and ineffective. The Philippines has been unable to
negotiate with neighbours on overlapping maritime jurisdictions on anything
like a sound footing. These consequences have everything to do with people's
lives and communities — the integrity of the marine ecology, the ability to
fish, the availability of energy resources, the capacity of the sea to sustain life
in its many forms, the responsibility for search and rescue in case of maritime
accidents, the safety and viability of coastal communities, and so on.

There are no easy answers to the questions raised at the beginning of this
chapter. There are no obvious positions that the Philippine government ought
to take. This book does not suggest answers; it raises questions, hopefully
the right ones. Nor does it go into the intricate legal arguments that are
the province of scholars much more learned than I am. It is not meant for
specialists but for Filipinos concerned over a vital issue in their national life
and for others who are interested in a fascinating case of geography's role in
a nation's history and development. What this book does is try to illuminate
the many complex issues involved and urge the country to make up its mind
on the positions to take on them; that is, at last, definitively to define the
extent of the Philippine national territory and maritime jurisdiction. This
requires overcoming the tendency of politicians to defer the resolution of these
difficult and explosive issues to the next administration or the next legislature;
in other words, it demands national leadership of the highest order.

First, the book reviews the measures taken by the colonial powers — Spain,
the United States, and both of them together — and by the pre-independence
Philippines, including in the 1935 Constitution, to define the extent of the
Philippines' territory and jurisdiction, unilaterally and through agreements
with other countries. Among the considerations taken into account was the
difficult relationship of the Muslim Filipinos with the colonial powers and
with the rest of the country. The book then examines such definitions in the
1973 and 1987 Constitutions and in various pertinent pieces of legislation and

international agreements and how they resolve the territorial and jurisdictional questions — or fail to do so or even complicate them. The book summarizes the nature of the Philippine claim to Sabah and discusses its implications for the territorial and jurisdictional issues. A whole host of maritime questions are discussed, with the South China Sea being treated more extensively and in greater detail in a separate chapter. Much of this is done in the light of the UNCLOS, which the Philippines ratified but on which it issued a declaration, made upon signature and reiterated upon ratification, but challenged by others as not allowed under the UNCLOS. Finally, the book makes a point of stressing the necessity for the nation to resolve definitively, first within itself and then by agreement with others involved, the country's territorial and maritime jurisdiction, recognising the obstacles to such a determination and pointing to the consequences of leaving things undecided.

The occasional duplication between chapters results from the intention to allow readers to read individual chapters by themselves.

Unless an endnote indicates otherwise, primary sources cited are compiled in Raphael Perpetuo Lotilla, ed., *The Philippine National Territory: A Collection of Related Documents* (Diliman, Quezon City: Institute of International Legal Studies, University of the Philippines Law Center, and Manila: Foreign Service Institute, Department of Foreign Affairs, 1995) or in *The Philippine Claim to a Portion of North Borneo: Materials and Documents* (Diliman, Quezon City: Institute of International Legal Studies, University of the Philippines Law Center, 2003).

This book was written when I was a Visiting Senior Research Fellow at the Institute of Southeast Asian Studies (ISEAS) in Singapore and, subsequently, head of the ASEAN Studies Centre at ISEAS. It was made possible by a grant to ISEAS from the Carlos P. Romulo Foundation for Peace and Development. I am thus especially grateful to the foundation and its chairman, Roberto R. Romulo, son of the great Philippine diplomat and himself a former Philippine foreign minister. My gratitude goes to Andres Soriano III and to the Zuellig Group, chaired by Dr Stephen Zuellig, both major donors to the grant.

I deeply appreciate the leadership of K. Kesavapany, director of ISEAS, for immediately seeing the value of a book on this subject. I am greatly indebted to the meticulously sharp work of Triena Ong and her staff at ISEAS' Publications Unit.

I am also grateful to those who furnished me with data and shared their valuable insights with me. I wish to make special mention of Henry Bensurto, Secretary-General of the Commission on Maritime and Ocean Affairs of the Philippines, who clarified numerous points pertaining to the latest developments in Philippine maritime policy, and his immediate superior, Undersecretary of Foreign Affairs Rafael Seguis. Similar thanks go to Ambassador Victoriano Lecaors, Philippine envoy to Malaysia, and to Ambassador Luis T. Cruz, former Minister-Counsellor in the Philippine embassy in Kuala Lumpur and later ambassador to the Republic of Korea. I thank the anonymous referee who made many useful suggestions, most of which I have incorporated in the manuscript.

I, of course, deeply appreciate the foreword contributed by a friend and colleague, Professor Dr Hasjim Djalal, retired Indonesian ambassador and moving spirit behind the continuing series of informal workshops on managing potential conflict in the South China Sea. A former vice-chairman of the Indonesian delegation to the 3rd UN Law of the Sea Conference, he is one of the world's leading authorities on maritime issues.

Needless to say, any errors and other shortcomings in this book can be attributed only to me.

Finally, and not least, I wish to thank my wife, Weng, for the forbearance that she bestowed on me while I was doing the research on and writing this work.

2

THE COLONIAL LEGACY

Before the Spanish exploration and conquest of what was to become the Philippines, most of the people of the islands lived in *barangays*, communities named after the boats in which their ancestors are said to have sailed from across the seas. Although such communities were, individually or in groups, self-governing, with no archipelago-wide central authority to which they owed allegiance, they shared similar cultures, customs, languages and traditions, and groups of them were often bound together by family ties or common interests or both.

The centuries-long process of consolidating the islands and seas of the Philippines into a national community and eventually a national state did not begin until Spanish explorers and *conquistadores* arrived in the sixteenth century. This process was accompanied — and reinforced — by the steady development of a sense of nationhood among the Filipinos themselves.

In May 1493, in an attempt to put some order into the scramble for territories between the two leading maritime powers at the time, Spain and Portugal, the Spanish-born Pope Alexander VI issued a Bull granting to the Spanish sovereigns, Ferdinand and Isabela, "all islands and mainlands found and to be found, discovered and to be discovered towards the west and south" of a line drawn from the North Pole to the South Pole 100 leagues from the Azores and Cape Verde islands (off West Africa) except for lands under Christian possession as of Christmas 1492.[1] (The marriage of Ferdinand and Isabela in 1469 had brought together the kingdoms of Aragón and Castille, forming the foundation of present-day Spain.)

In June 1494, the Spanish sovereigns and the Portuguese King concluded the Treaty of Tordesillas, confirmed by Pope Julius II in 1506, which moved the demarcation line westwards to 370 leagues west of the Azores and Cape

Verde islands. Portugal and Spain had initiated the age of European exploration and colonization of the Americas, Africa, the coasts of South Asia, and island Southeast Asia, to be followed by the Dutch and the British. In 1542, Charles V, Holy Roman Emperor and ruler of the Spanish realms, whose maternal grandparents were Ferdinand and Isabela, decided to colonize what was to become the Philippines. The colonization of the Philippines began in earnest with the establishment by the *adelantado* Miguel López de Legazpi of Spanish settlements on various islands, starting in 1565 and reaching a high point with the founding of the city of Manila in 1571. This took place under the auspices of King Philip II, who had succeeded his father Charles upon the latter's abdication in 1556 and after whom the archipelago was later to be named.

THE COMING OF SPAIN

The first prominent European to set foot on Philippine soil, on 16 March 1521, was Ferdinand Magellan. In the service of the Spanish king, this intrepid Portuguese naval leader had set sail for the Spice Islands, east of Europe, by going west. The expedition had started out with five ships but, on account of one wreck and one desertion, wound up with only three when it found the island of Homonhon, near Cebu. Magellan's fleet was the first to circumnavigate the world. However, he himself was killed by Lapu Lapu on the nearby island of Mactan while doing battle with the Mactan chieftain and his men on behalf of the Cebu leader, Rajah Humabon, who had become Magellan's friend and a convert to Christianity. Only one ship, with eighteen men on board, managed to return to Spain.

Because the Philippines was a collection of islands, it was found necessary, more than 370 years later, to designate, by cartographic coordinates, what was being ceded by Spain to the United States. This was done in the Treaty of Peace signed in Paris on 10 December 1898 to end the Spanish-American War of that year.

THE 1898 SPAIN-U.S. PEACE TREATY

In 1896, the *Katipunan ng Mga Anak ng Bayan* (Society of the Children of the Nation), a secret society espousing Filipino interests, had launched an armed revolution against Spain, which had been expanding its rule over the Philippines since the sixteenth century. Led by Andrés Bonifacio, a working-class revolutionary, the Katipunan embodied long-simmering Filipino grievances that had occasionally erupted into armed revolt during the some 333 years of Spanish rule. With the revolution gaining strength and rapidly spreading, its leadership was taken over by a faction headed by Emilio Aguinaldo, who was then twenty-eight years old. A revolutionary government superseded the Katipunan and, following a power struggle, executed Bonifacio for "treason". As the hostilities between the Filipinos and the Spaniards wore on with no clear victor, Aguinaldo concluded, in December 1897, an armistice with the Spanish governor-general, under which Aguinaldo would go into exile in Hong Kong and receive "$800,000 (Mexican)" in exchange for the surrender of a certain quantity of arms.

In April 1898, the Spanish-American War broke out, involving Cuba, Puerto Rico and the Philippines. As part of that war, the U.S. Asiatic Squadron under the command of Commodore, later Admiral, George Dewey set sail from China to Manila Bay. On the eve of the war, Aguinaldo, in exile in Hong Kong, had received two emissaries from the commander of the USS *Petrel*, who urged him to return to the Philippines to resume the fight against the Spaniards "with the object of gaining our independence". Although Dewey's squadron sank or captured all the Spanish warships, took out Spain's armaments on shore and had Spanish Manila under his guns, he did not have the land troops to occupy the city. According to Aguinaldo,[2] the *Petrel* commander assured him of American assistance, declaring, "The United States is a great and rich nation and needs no colonies." Aguinaldo left Hong Kong on 7 April 1898 and, after a stop in Saigon, arrived in Singapore two weeks later. Upon his Singapore landfall, Aguinaldo received the American consul, Spencer Pratt, who informed him that Dewey had sent a telegram giving assurances of U.S. recognition of Philippine independence "under the protection of the U.S. Navy". In response to Aguinaldo's query, Pratt stressed that there was no need for a formal written agreement, as "the word of the Admiral and of the United States Consul were in fact equivalent to the most solemn pledge that their verbal promises and assurance would be fulfilled to the letter". "Placing the fullest confidence in their word of honour", Aguinaldo assured Pratt that he would lead the resumed fight against the Spaniards. Upon Dewey's advice, Aguinaldo returned to Hong Kong, where, together with the American consul in Hong Kong, Rounseville Wildman, he boarded the American despatch boat *McCulloch* for the voyage to the Philippines. The *McCulloch* arrived in Manila Bay on 19 May. On board the admiral's flagship, the USS *Olympia*, Dewey, according to Aguinaldo, confirmed what Pratt had told the Filipino general, "adding that the United States had come to the Philippines to protect the natives and free them from the yoke of Spain. He said, moreover, that America is exceedingly well off as regards territory, revenue, and resources and therefore needs no colonies, assuring me finally that there was no occasion for me to entertain any doubts whatever about the recognition of the Independence of the Philippines by the United States." On 4 July, the first U.S. military expedition, under General Anderson, landed at Cavite, across the bay from Manila. Again according to Aguinaldo, "General Anderson solemnly and completely endorsed the promises made by Admiral Dewey to me, asserting on his word of honour that America had not come to the Philippines to wage war against the natives nor to conquer and retain territory, but only to liberate the people from the oppression of the Spanish Government."

Dewey was later to deny having given those assurances. In any case, on 12 June 1898, with the Spanish forces defeated all over the country, Philippine independence was proclaimed at Aguinaldo's house in the town of Kawit, not far from Manila, the new Philippine flag was unfurled, and the Philippine national anthem was played publicly for the first time. Ominously, Dewey declined to attend the ceremonies, but the text of the independence proclamation referred to the presence of the only foreigner, one L. M. Johnson, identified as an American Colonel of Artillery. The proclamation expressed the Filipinos' "profound gratitude" to the United States "for its disinterested protection which it lent us and continues lending us". However, Washington, as well as Spain, refused to recognize the Philippines' proclaimed independence. Indeed, two months after the proclamation, U.S. military contingents entered Manila, having agreed with the Spanish governor-general that Spanish forces would surrender to the Americans and not to the Filipinos and that the U.S. troops would prevent Philippine fighters from entering Manila. The Filipinos' sense of betrayal — and naïveté — and the North Americans' perceived duplicity and determination to keep their new colonial foothold in Asia led directly to the Philippine-American War of 1899–1902, which many Americans insist on calling the Philippine "insurrection" to this day.

Meanwhile, Apolinario Mabini, known as the brains of the Philippine revolution, was working on a constitution for the Philippines in anticipation of the country's independence. His Constitutional Programme of the Philippine Republic, which laid down the elements that he thought should go into the new constitution, defined, in Title II, the territory of the republic:

> 20. The Philippine Republic is the group of all Filipinos residing in the territory made up of the islands of Luzon, Visayas and Mindanao, the Jolo archipelago and other adjacent islands within the region formerly known by the name of Philippine Islands.

> The Marianas Islands, the Carolines and other territories subject to the Spanish Government in the Oceania region shall form an integral part of

the Philippine Republic, if they voluntarily make common cause with the Filipinos in the pursuit of their independence.[3]

However, as worked out by a convention in the town of Malolos north of Manila and as Aguinaldo promulgated it in January 1899, the Malolos Constitution contained, like most other constitutions, no definition of the national territory. It did provide for the separation of church and state, the separation of powers among the executive, legislative and judicial branches, and the guarantee of human rights.[4] Mabini went on to become Prime Minister and Minister of Foreign Affairs of the short-lived republic.

In October 1898, Spain and the United States had started negotiating in Paris a treaty ending the war between them. Under the treaty, Spain relinquished sovereignty over and title to Cuba. It provided for the U.S. occupation of that island and ceded Puerto Rico, Guam and the Philippines from Spain to the United States. Ignoring the Philippines' assertion of the victory of its independence revolution and the entreaties of the Philippine envoy in Paris, Felipe Agoncillo, Spanish and American plenipotentiaries signed the treaty on 10 December 1898.

It was only in the case of the Philippines that the Treaty of Paris, in its Article III, defined the limits of the territory being ceded:

Spain cedes to the United States the archipelago known as the Philippine Islands, and comprehending the islands lying within the following line:

A line running from west to east along or near the twentieth parallel of north latitude, and through the middle of the navigable channel of Bachi, from the one hundred and eighteenth (118th) to the one hundred and twenty-seventh (127th) degree meridian of longitude east of Greenwich, thence along the one hundred and twenty seventh (127th) degree meridian of longitude east of Greenwich to the parallel of four degrees and forty five minutes (4°45') north latitude, thence along the parallel of four degrees and forty five minutes (4°45') north latitude to its intersection with the meridian of longitude one hundred and nineteen degrees and thirty five minutes (119°35') east of Greenwich, thence along the meridian of longitude one hundred and nineteen degrees and thirty five minutes (119°35') east of Greenwich to the parallel of latitude seven degrees and forty minutes (7°40') north, thence along the parallel of latitude of seven degrees and forty minutes (7°40') north to its intersection with the one hundred and sixteenth (116th) degree meridian of longitude east of Greenwich, thence by a direct line to the intersection of the tenth (10th) degree parallel of north latitude with the one hundred and eighteenth (118th) degree meridian of longitude east of Greenwich, and thence along the one hundred and eighteenth (118th) degree meridian of longitude east of Greenwich to the point of beginning. The United States will pay to Spain the sum of twenty million dollars ($20,000,000) within three months after the exchange of the ratifications of the present treaty.[5]

The U.S. Senate approved the ratification of the treaty by only one vote more than the required two-thirds majority on 6 February 1899, two days after an American sentry in a Manila suburb fired the first shot of the Philippine-American War.

The Philippine territory being ceded by Spain to the United States had to be defined, evidently because the Philippines, unlike Puerto Rico or Guam, was not a land mass whose contours were clear but a sprawling archipelago of scattered islands. Some outlying islands could be subject to claims by neighbouring powers if their inclusion in Philippine territory remained unclear; for example, The Netherlands and the United Kingdom in the south and Japan, which had just occupied nearby Taiwan, in the north. Senator Arturo Tolentino, in sponsoring the first bill that sought to define the baselines of the Philippines' territorial sea, gave another reason for this. He told the Philippine Senate in May 1960 that, "during the treaty negotiations, Spain was trying to hide some islands or islands not to be ceded". "So," he continued, "the United States insisted in (sic) the drawing of the boundaries and everything within that is (sic) ceded."[6]

The United States found it necessary to conclude, on 7 November 1900, another treaty with Spain, in which Madrid explicitly ceded to the United States the Spanish islands lying outside the limits set by the Treaty of Paris, including specifically Cagayan (de Sulu), Sulu and Sibutu. The lone article of the 1900 treaty read in part:

> Spain relinquishes to the United States all title and claim of title, which she may have had at the time of the conclusion of the Treaty of Peace of Paris, to any and all islands belonging to the Philippine Archipelago, lying outside the lines described in Article III of that Treaty and particularly to the islands of Cagayan, Sulu and Sibutu and their dependencies, and agrees that all such islands shall be comprehended in the cession of the Archipelago as fully as if they had been expressly included within those lines.[7]

The 1900 treaty also provided for the payment of a further $100,000 by the United States to Spain, in addition to the $20 million that the Washington had committed to Madrid under the 1898 Treaty of Paris.

MINDANAO AND SULU

Although Mindanao, Sulu and related islands were encompassed within the territorial limits set for the Philippines by the Spain-U.S. treaties of 1898 and 1900, the sultanates of Maguindanao and Sulu and the other sultanates, numerous datuships and other Islamic dominions in the archipelago's south had for centuries after Spain's arrival in the Philippines acted like sovereign states rather than as territories subject to Spanish rule. They formed alliances and pursued rivalries among themselves and with the Dutch and the British to the south and with the Spaniards who sought to colonize them from the north. They engaged in commerce, including trade in arms and slaves, and entered into treaties, including with the United States. The Sulu sultanate sent missions to and exchanged gifts with the Chinese emperor in Beijing. Despite their forts in such outposts as Zamboanga and Tamontaca and their scattered settlements in Mindanao and Sulu, the Spaniards never succeeded in subjugating all the Muslim polities at the same time. On the contrary, it was often the Muslims who laid siege to the Spanish forts and settlements in their midst and conducted raids in northern and eastern Mindanao, the Visayas and even parts of Luzon, raids carried out either in reprisal or for material gain or both.[8] There were also the non-Muslim tribes in Mindanao, some of them converted to Christianity, who pursued their own self-interest through trade and warfare.[9] The Muslim and other tribal communities continued to conduct their affairs in this way until the early years of the American occupation.

In April 1851, having fled a Spanish onslaught that culminated in the colonizers' capture of the Sulu capital, Jolo, Sultan Mohammed Pulalun had to sign a treaty with Spain, which, according to the Spaniards, placed Sulu under Spanish sovereignty as part of the Philippine islands. It forbade Sulu from entering into treaties, trade agreements or alliances with other European powers, corporations or persons or with Malay chieftains. It promised regular payments to the Sultan and his datus. It obliged Sulu to refrain from constructing forts without the express permission of the Spanish Governor-General and to prohibit the purchase or use of firearms without a licence from the Spanish authorities. In turn, the Spanish government would assure the Sultan and the inhabitants of Sulu freedom of religion and respect for their customs. Sulu saw things differently. According to its Tausug version, the treaty merely called for a Spanish protectorate over Sulu. The Spanish version, however, stated that the Spanish text would prevail in case of doubt.[10]

In May 1861, Sultan Jamalul Kiram of Sulu sought the help of the British Governor of Singapore and Malacca, insisting that Sulu had cooperated with Spain in the suppression of piracy, as the 1851 treaty called for, but complaining that the sums promised had not been paid and that Spain was preventing traders from entering Sulu. However, the British politely turned down the appeal for help.[11]

In 1876, the Spanish authorities went on another successful offensive against Jolo. The treaty that Sultan Jamalul Alam signed with Spain in July 1878 had the same apparent inconsistency between the two texts as the 1851 pact, but without the provision that the Spanish text would prevail in case of disagreement. According to the Spanish version, the 1878 treaty recognized Spanish sovereignty over the Sulu archipelago and its dependencies and explicitly affirmed the right of Spain to occupy points in Sulu and its dependencies. It obliged the Sultan and his datus to stop pirates and other "malefactors" from carrying out their "evil intentions" and, failing that, to inform the Spanish Governor of Sulu accordingly, so that he could take his own measures. While assuring the Muslims of the freedom to practise their religion and customs, the treaty allowed Catholic missionaries to reside in and visit any point in Sulu and its dependencies. It provided for much higher salaries for the Sultan, the Raja Muda, the Raja Laut and the two other datus who signed the treaty.[12]

Desperate for help and for funds, the Sultan had agreed in January 1878 to a proposal by the Austrian Gustavus Baron de Overbeck and the Briton Alfred Dent, "as representatives of a British Company", that the land in North Borneo belonging to Sulu be "leased" to them "forever and until the end of time" and "for as long as they choose or desire to use them". In return, Overbeck and Dent promised to pay the Sultan and his heirs and successors "five thousand dollars annually".[13] The Filipino Jesuit historian Horacio de la Costa, S. J., asks, "But what exactly did the Sultan of Sulu make over to the North Borneo Company by this instrument? What did the word *padjak* mean in the original text? Did it mean, as the British translation has it, a grant or cession? Or did it mean a lease? Assuming that it was a grant, did the Company acquire property rights only, or also political sovereignty? The time would come when these would be questions of some importance."[14] De la Costa was referring to the Philippines' forthcoming claim to North Borneo, discussed at length in Chapter 4.

Although the Muslim sultans and datus and the rulers of the non-Muslim tribes in the southern Philippines did not consider themselves as having been under Spanish rule — or, indeed, as part of the new nation that had risen in revolt against Spain — Mindanao, Sulu and related islands were included in the territory transferred by Spain to the United States in the 1898 Treaty of Paris and in the 1900 agreement between the two countries. While the Americans had their hands full fighting a war with the Filipinos in Luzon, the Visayas and eastern and northern Mindanao, they tried to buy some time by avoiding having to fight on a second front — the Muslims and others in Mindanao and Sulu — with undermanned forces. They did this through the instrumentality of the Bates Treaty, which Brigadier General John C. Bates, an American government emissary, signed with Sultan Jamalul Kiram II of Sulu and four datus in August 1899, an agreement based on the 1878 treaty between Spain and Sulu.

As in the case of Spain and Sulu in the 1878 document, there was a difference in interpretation or perception between the two sides as to whether the Bates Treaty provided for full American sovereignty or merely a protectorate over Sulu and its dependencies. On the one hand, Article I stated that the "sovereignty of the United States over the whole archipelago of Jolo and its dependencies is declared and acknowledged", and Article II provided for the use of the U.S. flag there. On the other hand, the purchase of land in the archipelago would be subject to the Sultan's consent (but registered with the U.S. Government). Crimes of Muslims against other Muslims would be tried and punished by "the government of the Sultan". Article XIII obliged the United States to "give full protection to the Sultan and his subjects in case any foreign nation should attempt to impose upon them". If the United States had sovereignty over the Sulu territories, why conclude a treaty with their ruler explicitly providing for his and his subjects' protection? This question could have given rise to the argument that the Bates Treaty only established an American protectorate over Sulu. Like the 1878 agreement, the treaty granted the Muslims autonomy in matters of religion and religious customs. The Sultan was to be paid a monthly salary of 250 Mexican dollars, and nine other Muslim chiefs were to be given amounts ranging from 15 to 75 Mexican dollars a month. Sulu or any part of it was not to be sold to any other country without the Sultan's consent, a provision that gave rise to deep resentment among Muslims when Sulu was included in the Philippine nation to which the United States granted independent sovereignty in 1946.[15]

Peter G. Gowing, then Director of the Dansalan Research Center at Dansalan College in Marawi City, Philippines, was to observe:

> The American authorities in 1899 seemed to be unaware of the significance of their seeking to step directly into the shoes of the Spaniards in Moroland. What they had in mind was to get Moro acknowledgement of the fact that the United States had succeeded to the status of sovereign in Moroland. But the Americans did not seem to understand that the Treaty of 1878 had been, from the viewpoint of the Sulu Moros, nothing more than a *modus vivendi* with Spain, the limits of which the Moros were constantly testing. The emoluments paid by Spain to the Sultan were regarded by him as something in the nature of tribute in exchange for his "co-operation" in keeping the Sulus peaceful. Again from the Moro viewpoint, the United States in 1899 was seeking to occupy exactly the same irritating position

that Spain had held in Sulu but which the Moros had learned to live with
and to circumvent as conditions permitted. The Americans little realized
that in seeking to step into Spanish shoes they were likely also to inherit
Spain's problems with the Moros.[16]

Early in their occupation of the Philippines, the Americans sought to draw
Sulu and Mindanao into the emerging Philippine body politic and rule them
directly instead of indirectly, through their traditional rulers, as the British were
doing in Malaya through the Malay rulers and the Dutch in the East Indies
through the Javanese and other sultans. They would bring the non-Christian
communities under the same set of laws and administrative arrangements as
the rest of the Philippines. As part of this effort, General George W. Davis,
Commander of the Department of Mindanao and Sulu, recommended, as
early as October 1901, the abrogation of the Bates Treaty, the withdrawal
of the authority of the Sultan over all the Moros, the recognition of datus
merely as "headmen" who would be paid only if they actually performed
public service, and the trial by government courts of all capital offenses and
cases of slavery regardless of the religion of the accused or the victim. These
recommendations formed the basis of the Act adopted in June 1903 by the
Philippine Commission, the body temporarily administering the Philippines
at that time, providing for direct American rule over a new civilian Moro
Province, creating its administrative subdivisions, guiding its transition from
military to civilian rule, and prescribing its manner of governance.[17]

However, the Bates Treaty remained formally in force. In July 1903, Davis
again criticized that agreement as "an obstacle to the establishment of good
government" and urged its abrogation. Brigadier General Samuel Sumner,
who had succeeded Davis as Commander of the U.S. Army's Department of
Mindanao, supported his predecessor's recommendations, citing the "anarchy"
prevailing in Sulu, the difficulty of bringing the Muslims under American law,
and the inability of the Sultan to carry out his obligations under the treaty.

Major General Leonard Wood, the first Governor of Moro Province and
Sumner's successor as Commander of the Department of Mindanao, added his
influential voice to the call for the abrogation of the Bates Treaty, denigrating
the character of the Mindanao and Sulu Muslims and of the Sultan himself
and accusing them of "bad faith". In support of the recommendations that
he submitted in December 1903 to Governor-General William Howard Taft,
Wood charged that the Sultan's administration was corrupt and arbitrary and
tolerated the killing of American soldiers and the theft of U.S. property. He
called Muslim laws cruel and barbaric, singling out the practice of slavery.
Wood stressed that, because he actually had little power over the datus, the

Sultan was unable or unwilling to live up to his obligations under the Bates Treaty. He concluded that the treaty was incompatible with the sovereignty that he said Spain had transferred to the United States. Taft endorsed Wood's recommendations.[18]

Accordingly, on 2 March 1904, U.S. President Theodore Roosevelt unilaterally abrogated the Bates Treaty. The United States also stopped the payments to the Sultan and the datus. (The payments were soon restored.) General Wood informed Sultan Jamalul Kiram II of this development nineteen days later. In an April 1904 letter to Luke E. Wright, who had succeeded Taft as Governor-General that year, the Sultan, in terms that were dripping with a combination of self-pity and indignation, protested against the unilateral nature of the Bates Treaty's abrogation, the imposition of taxes on the Moro people, and the compulsion on them to do acts that, according to him, were contrary to Islam. He insisted that he had complied with the treaty, citing the help that he had extended to the United States in the fight against the rebellion of Panglima Hassan in October 1903. He acquiesced in the liberation of slaves but asked for payment for their loss. The Sultan pleaded for the retention of his authority in four matters that he claimed belonged to him by virtue of the tenets of his religion — marital quarrels and divorce, marriage and child custody, inheritance, and the appointment of religious authorities. He accepted the removal of his "temporal power and rights" as long as he was compensated for the loss and appealed for the retention of his leadership of the Moros and of the "contributions due me as such".[19]

It is not surprising that fierce fighting continued — and even intensified — between the Americans and the sultanates and datuships of Mindanao and Sulu, individually or in transitory alliances. The conflict between the Muslims and the Americans was exacerbated by the American drive to bring the sultanates and datuships under direct rule, threatening and often taking away the powers and incomes of the sultans and the datus. Claiming that Spain never had sovereignty over their people and their lands (a claim that the Carpenter Agreement, below, was to acknowledge) and, therefore, had no right to hand them over to the United States, many Muslims resisted the imposition on them of American laws and new taxes and the distribution of their lands to Christian Filipinos and others. Especially rankling were the Americans' prohibition of slavery, a form of wealth in Mindanao and Sulu, and the removal from the Muslim rulers of the power to try crimes of Muslims against Muslims — and collect the fines. Fundamental to these animosities was the direct conflict between, on the one hand, the American approach to administration and government on the theoretical basis of the rule of law and the equality of all before the law — religions as well as men — and, on the other hand, the hierarchical structure of the Muslim sultanates and datuships on the basis of family and other personal ties, hereditary succession, class divisions and religious tenets. This was, of course, in addition to law-and-order problems, like the theft of cattle, slavery, the illegal possession of weapons, piracy, and blood and family feuds, on which the American regime sought to enforce American-enacted laws, and to the American efforts generally to subdue the Muslims and other tribes of Mindanao and Sulu by force of arms.

In 1913, a new Democratic administration under President Woodrow Wilson assumed office in Washington, D.C. It sought to civilianize the government of the Philippines — and expand Filipino participation in it — with a view to accelerating the country's eventual independence. Part of this effort was the transformation of the military-administered Moro Province, whose first three Governors were military generals, to the civilian Department of Mindanao and Sulu, where almost all national laws were to take effect.

In March 1915, Frank Carpenter, the last Governor of Moro Province and the first Governor of the Department of Mindanao and Sulu, concluded with the Sultan of Sulu another treaty, known as the Carpenter Agreement. Seeking to make its basic purpose clear, the agreement was titled "the Complete Renunciation by the Latter (the Sultan of Sulu) of his Pretensions of Sovereignty and a Definition of his Status". It noted that, before the American occupation, "the Sultanate of Sulu had been for more than 400 years an independent sovereignty". It recalled that the Bates Treaty had referred to the "Government of the Sultan", which had the power to try crimes of Moros against other Moros. The new agreement did not abolish the sultanate but recognized the Sultan only as the "spiritual head of the Mohameddan Church in the Sulu Archipelago", with the same rights and privileges as the heads of other religions under American jurisdiction, as well as the same limitations on those rights and privileges. It affirmed the Sultan's "recognition of the sovereignty" of the United States, specifically including the right and power of government courts and other authorized officials to adjudicate *all* civil and criminal cases. Finally, it established religious freedoms that were "not in violation of the basic principles of the laws of the United States of America".[20]

President Wilson, his appointed Governor-General for the Philippines, Francis Burton Harrison, a fellow-Democrat from New York, and Carpenter, had been accelerating the Filipinization policy initiated by their Republican predecessors. Together with the influx of Christian Filipinos from the northern provinces into Mindanao, this resulted in the domination by Christian Filipinos of the municipal and provincial, as well as the central, governments of the

Philippines and other loci of power, including the Philippine Scouts and the Constabulary. These trends alarmed the Muslims, who felt that they were being subordinated to their erstwhile enemies and feared that their religion would be brought under pressure. Indeed, although at the personal level much friendly interaction took place between Christian and Muslim Filipinos, some of the Muslims are said to have expressed their preference for continued American administration and, in any case, an existence for their lands and domains separate from the Filipino nation.[21] In the event, the 1898 and 1900 treaties between the United States and Spain had formalized the geographic unity of the Philippine archipelago, whose political integrity came to be embedded in both the Filipino psyche, with the exception of some Muslim Filipinos, and American policy.

On 2 January 1930, the United States and the United Kingdom signed the Washington Convention, which sought to clarify and set the boundary between the Philippines and "the State of North Borneo which is under British protection" (not sovereignty). The agreement laid down the geographical lines between the territory ceded by Spain to the United States under the 1898 and 1900 treaties and British North Borneo.[22] However, as is discussed in Chapter 4 of this book, this has not prevented the Philippines from claiming sovereignty over North Borneo territory on the grounds that the Sultanate of Sulu had not given up sovereignty over its territories in North Borneo and had ceded them to the Philippine Republic. On the same day, the U.S. and British governments exchanged notes specifying that "the sovereignty over certain islands which have for many years past been administered by the British North Borneo Company has been definitely recognized as pertaining to the United States of America". The islands referred to were the Turtle and Mangsee Islands. However, the British North Borneo Company was to continue administering the islands until the United States asked for the transfer of their administration.[23] In September 1946, shortly after it regained its independence, the Philippines sought to assume the administration of those islands, to which the British agreed. The transfer took effect about a year later.

Notwithstanding these treaties, conventions and other legal documents, it was — and remains — easy to ignore the boundaries that they laid down, however one was to interpret them. After all, unlike many of those drawn on land, boundaries on the sea are invisible except on the maps of the learned. Accordingly, the Sulu Sea is less a barrier than a highway for people to cross from Tawi Tawi, Sulu, Basilan, Zamboanga and beyond to Sabah and from Sabah to Mindanao and the islands to its south — for reasons of religion, family visits, security, trade and employment. In this light, the large numbers of Filipinos living in Sabah and of Indonesians resident in Mindanao should not be surprising to anyone, regardless of what the maps and the laws and agreements say.

During the debate on the provision on the national territory in the 1972 Constitution, one delegate to the 1971–72 Constitutional Convention, E. Voltaire Garcia II, was to claim that the inclusion of such an explicit provision in the 1935 Constitution had been motivated by fears that the United States would retain some Philippine islands as a permanent colony or as trust territories.[24] This claim was reiterated by some members of the Constitutional Commission that drafted the 1987 Constitution. For example, Regalado Maambong declared on 30 June 1986 that the provision on the national territory had been inserted in the 1935 Constitution in order to prevent the "dismemberment" of the Philippines by the United States.[25] The next day, Joaquin Bernas, S. J., said much the same thing.[26]

Those fears had been stoked by a number of proposals to keep Mindanao and Sulu apart from the emergent Filipino nation. As early as 1905, Gowing recalls, "the Zamboanga Chamber of Commerce, made up mostly of American businessmen, presented a resolution to Secretary of War William Howard Taft and several visiting U.S. Congressmen" asking "that Mindanao and Sulu be formed into a territory of the United States by Act of Congress". Colonel Ralph W. Hoyt, then Acting Governor of Moro Province, recommended in 1909 the "permanent separation as early as possible" of Mindanao, Sulu, Palawan and adjacent islands from the Philippine archipelago as an American colony named the Mindanao Plantation.[27] In 1926, Robert Low Bacon, Republican from New York, filed a bill in the U.S. House of Representatives seeking to separate Mindanao and Sulu from the rest of the Philippines. Apparently not being part of official U.S. policy, these attempts failed but continued to haunt Filipinos for many years.

BATANES

In August 1934, Nicolás Buendia, chairman of the nine-man Committee on Territorial Delimitation of the Constitutional Convention that was drafting the 1935 Philippine Constitution, wrote a letter to the convention seeking to correct an "error" in the Treaty of Paris that would appear to exclude the Batanes islands from Philippine territory. Buendia's letter said:

> According to this delimitation (having quoted the pertinent description of the Philippines' northern limits in the Treaty of Paris), the beautiful Batanes Islands, which since time immemorial have been an integral part of the Philippine Islands, are not included in our territory.

It is true that in speaking of the line running from west to east near the 20th parallel of the north longitude (sic), mention is also made of the navigable Channel of Bashi (Bachi), which is the real boundary through which said line passes, and according to this, the Batanes Islands are within our territory; but it is no less true that said Channel does not and cannot coincide with the 20th parallel of the north latitude but with that of 21°25'N. Hence, a line running from the west to east near the 20th parallel of the north latitude would pass not through the Bashi Channel but through the Balintang Channel.

This erroneous description appearing in the Treaty of Paris was no doubt taken from the data on file in the archives of the Spanish Government and it is to be supposed that this error in the degree dates back to the Spanish regime.

In order to correct that error and avoid all possibility of confusion in the future regarding the real boundaries of our territory towards the north, your Committee has changed the erroneous 20th parallel of north latitude to 21°25'V. , making it coincide perfectly with the Bashi Channel, which is the real boundary.[28]

Buendia also sought to exclude Palmas island, or Miangas, from the Constitution's definition of the national territory, citing the fact that an arbitrator, Max Huber, had awarded the island to The Netherlands in 1928. The Dutch and the Americans had agreed to submit their dispute over the island to arbitration. According to Buendia, the inclusion of Palmas/Miangas in the Treaty of Paris limits was a mistake. As successor-state to The Netherlands, Indonesia took over the island upon its independence.[29]

THE MARITIME JURISDICTION

The provision in the Treaty of Paris setting the limits and extent of the Philippines has been subsequently invoked in national and international debates on the country's national territory and maritime jurisdiction. However, the Treaty of Paris speaks merely of the Philippine archipelago and the islands within the limits that the treaty draws up. Having been concluded long before the United Nations Convention on the Law of the Sea and other international maritime conventions, it is silent on the nature of the maritime jurisdiction in the various expanses of water within those lines.

In December 1932, the U.S. Congress passed the Hare-Hawes-Cutting bill. Pushed by a protectionist farm sector fearing competition from Philippine sugar, cordage and coconut oil, the bill would impose tariffs and quotas on Philippine exports to the United States. It would reserve large tracts of

Philippine land for U.S. military reservations, grant self-government to the Philippines in a Commonwealth following the adoption of a constitution approved by the U.S. President, and restore independence to the Philippines on 4 July ten years after the Commonwealth's establishment. The Republican President, Herbert Hoover, vetoed the bill. Hoover argued that the too-early grant of independence would expose the Philippines to the designs of other foreign powers and damage the country's economy, while costing the United States greatly in strategic and economic terms. The U.S. Congress overrode the veto, but the Philippine Legislature, whose approval was required, rejected the bill.[30]

After a change in administration in the United States, the U.S. Congress in March 1934 approved an almost identical bill, filed by Maryland Senator Millard E. Tydings and Alabama Representative John McDuffie, both Democrats, which the Democratic President, Franklin D. Roosevelt, signed into law and the Philippine Legislature approved. The Tydings-McDuffie Act, like the Hare-Hawes-Cutting bill, provided that the Commonwealth "shall exercise jurisdiction over all the territory ceded to the United States by the treaty of peace concluded between the United States and Spain on the 10th day of December 1898, the *boundaries* (italics mine) of which are set forth in article III of said treaty, together with those islands embraced in the treaty between Spain and the United States concluded at Washington on the 7th day of November 1900". The use of the word "boundaries" seemed to reinforce the view that the sea between the islands of the Philippines and the lines drawn by the Treaty of Paris was part of the country's territorial waters, a view that was subsequently propounded on the basis of "legal and historic title" and on security and economic grounds.[31]

However, all this was taking place long before the 1982 UN Convention on the Law of the Sea defined more precisely the various kinds of maritime jurisdiction and the permissible ways of establishing them.

THE 1935 PHILIPPINE CONSTITUTION

The Treaty of Paris was specifically cited in the provision on the national territory in the 1935 Philippine Constitution, which was drafted and promulgated under American colonial rule but continued to govern the Philippines until the 1973 Constitution replaced it. Article I of the 1935 Constitution said:

> The Philippines comprises all the territory ceded to the United States by the Treaty of Paris concluded between the United States and Spain on the tenth day of December, eighteen hundred and ninety-eight, the limits of

which are set forth in Article III of said treaty, together with all the islands embraced in the treaty concluded at Washington between the United States and Spain on the seventh day of November, nineteen hundred, and the treaty concluded between the United States and Great Britain on the second day of January, nineteen hundred and thirty, and all territory over which the present Government of the Philippine Islands exercises jurisdiction.[32]

As pointed out in Chapter 3 of this book, a provision to define the national territory is unusual among national constitutions. Most national territories are determined by history and an accumulation of national laws and international treaties rather than by the country's constitution, which, in any case, is not binding on other nations. The Malolos Constitution, which the Philippine revolutionary government adopted in January 1899, had no provision defining the national territory. It only provided, in its Article 68, that a "special law" could authorize the President to "alienate, transfer or exchange any portion of Philippine territory" or to "incorporate any other territory to the Philippine territory".[33]

The 1934 Philippine Constitutional Convention held an elaborate debate on whether to include an article on the national territory in the 1935 Constitution. The debate was triggered by an amendment proposed by Wenceslao Q. Vinzons, at twenty-three the youngest delegate to the convention. He was later to become a guerrilla leader against the occupying Japanese forces and eventually to be executed by the Japanese. The Vinzons amendment sought to remove the article on the national territory from the draft Constitution. Another delegate, Jose M. Aruego, pointed out that a constitution should contain only the fundamental principles of government. Vicente Singson Encarnacion countered by asking where those fundamental principles would apply. The omission of the proposed article on the national territory, Aruego said, would "not deprive us of the territory we are entitled to; and its inclusion will not give us any territory of (sic) which in fact we have no title." Salvador Araneta was of the view that, by retaining the provision in question, the Constitution had to be amended should the Philippines acquire new territory. Mariano Jesús Cuenco cautioned that, by failing to define its territorial limits, the country would be opening itself both to charges of imperialistic intentions and to the possibility of separatism. He pointed to the growing Japanese presence in Davao and the proximity of the Philippines' northernmost islands to Japanese-occupied Taiwan as possible sources of the country's dismemberment if the national territory were not categorically defined in the Constitution. Singson Encarnacion and Ruperto Montinola argued that defining the national territory in the Constitution would erase all doubt about the extent of that territory. Gregorio Perfecto, for his part, cited the need for the Filipino people to know the territorial extent of their country and to proclaim to the world that they knew their own territory and that they had no desire to conquer other lands. In the end, the provision on the national territory was retained.

As we have seen, some of the stated reasons for the definition of the Philippine national territory in the 1935 Philippine Constitution were to make it explicitly clear that Mindanao and Sulu were part of the Philippines, forestall their retention by the United States after the rest of the Philippines had regained its independence, and prevent their secession from the country.

Like the Treaty of Paris, the 1935 Philippine Constitution, having been adopted well before the UNCLOS, did not spell out the nature of the maritime regimes around and between the Philippine islands or in the expanses of water within the limits set by the Treaty of Paris and described in the 1900 treaty between Spain and the United States.

THE DEBATE CONTINUES

Scholars have argued endlessly about this issue, including, in recent times, its relationship with the UNCLOS and that convention's ratification by the Philippines. At one extreme are Senator Miriam Defensor-Santiago and some law professors in the University of the Philippines. Their position is that everything within the lines drawn by the Treaty of Paris and subsequent international agreements is Philippine territory. The Chairman of the Senate Committee on Foreign Relations, Santiago has been quoted as asserting, "If the Philippines declares itself an archipelagic state, the declaration would contradict the Treaty of Paris which sets out the boundaries of our national territory, which are wider than those allowed by the UNCLOS."[34] However, she has later been quoted as saying that, while she was opposed to "surrendering our territorial claims", the "unacceptable choice is to claim as much territory as we want, alienate the rest of the international community, and operate as a pariah (under) international law".[35]

Indeed, several official Philippine documents antedating the UNCLOS declare that the waters between the outermost islands of the archipelago and the limits laid down by the Treaty of Paris are Philippine territory. For example, the fisheries law enacted in 1932 declared, in its Article II ("Definitions"), that the "waters pertaining to the Philippine Archipelago", as defined in the 1898 and 1900 Spain-U.S. treaties, were "territorial waters":

> "Philippine waters, or territorial waters of the Philippines", includes all waters pertaining to the Philippine Archipelago, as defined in the treaties between

the United States and Spain, dated respectively the tenth of December, eighteen hundred and ninety-eight, and the seventh of November, nineteen hundred.[36]

The 1961 law originally defining the baselines of the Philippines states in its preamble that "all the waters beyond the outermost islands of the archipelago but within the limits of the boundaries set forth in (the 1898 Treaty of Paris, the 1900 agreement between Spain and the United States, and the 1930 convention between the U.S. and the United Kingdom) comprise the territorial sea of the Philippines".[37] Several members of the Constitutional Commission that drew up the 1987 Constitution took the same position.

On the other side are those who favour adjusting the country's position on its territory, including its territorial and internal waters, its baselines, its contiguous zone, its exclusive economic zone, and its continental shelf, to accord as far as possible with the UNCLOS, which took effect well after the enactment of the 1932 fisheries law and the 1961 baselines act. This stand would be in line with the Philippines' ratification of the convention. It would mean rejecting the position that everything within the limits set by the Treaty of Paris is Philippine territory, water as well as land. Those who are of this view point out that no other state recognises the Treaty of Paris limits as legitimately enclosing any kind of maritime regime envisaged in the UNCLOS; not even the United States, which signed the Treaty of Paris, does so. Indeed, as early as January 1958, the United States took issue with a 1955 Philippine statement that all "water areas embraced in the imaginary lines described in the Treaty of Paris", the 1900 U.S.-Spain agreement, the 1930 convention between the United States and the United Kingdom, and Article I of the Philippine Constitution "are considered as maritime territorial waters of the Philippines". The U.S. Department of State declared, as an official position in response, that "the lines referred to in bilateral treaties between the United States and the United Kingdom and Spain merely delimited the area within which the land areas belong to the Philippines and that they were not intended as boundary lines".[38]

Between these two positions are a number of gradations and combinations of views on how the national territory is to be defined in the light not only of the country's security and economic requirements but also of the challenges posed, actually or potentially, by other states to the Philippines' positions and claims. Further complicating the discourse on the national territory are the Philippine claim to parts of North Borneo, which is dealt with in Chapter 4, the claim to some land features and waters of the South China Sea, which is discussed in Chapter 5, and, of course, the entry into force of the 1982

UN Convention on the Law of the Sea, to which the Philippines is a party, albeit with some qualifications.

The new Philippine baselines law, enacted in March 2009, seeks to make the definition of the country's maritime regime more compatible with the provisions of the UNCLOS. On the other hand, critics of that law insist that, by doing so, it has marked a retreat from the Philippine contention, made in the original baselines act and other documents, that the seas between the baselines around the main Philippine archipelago and the Treaty of Paris limits are Philippine territorial seas. A case challenging the constitutionality of the new baselines law has been filed with the Philippine Supreme Court.

Notes

1. <http://www.catholic-forum.com/saints/pope0214a.htm>.
2. The account in the rest of this paragraph draws from Don Emilio Aguinaldo y Famy, *True Version of the Philippine Revolution* (Tarlac, Philippines: 23 September 1899). Its English translation is found in <http://www.authorama.com/true-version-of-the-philippine-revolution-1.html>.
3. I am indebted to John Nery of the *Philippine Daily Inquirer* for bringing Mabini's Constitutional Programme to my attention. The translation from the Spanish is mine.
4. <http://www.chanrobles.com/1899constitutionofthephilippines.htm>.
5. Raphael Perpetuo M. Lotilla, ed., *The Philippine National Territory: A Collection of Related Documents* (Diliman, Quezon City: Institute of International Legal Studies, University of the Philippines Law Center, and Manila: Foreign Service Institute, Department of Foreign Affairs, 1995), p. 33. See Figure 1.
6. Ibid., p. 313.
7. Ibid., p. 38.
8. For highly readable accounts of this aspect of Spanish colonial rule and Mindanao and Sulu's resistance to it, see Ferdinand E. Marcos, *Tadhana: The History of the Filipino People*, Vol. 2, Part II (Manila: 1977), pp. 367–437, and Vol. 2, Part III (Manila: 1979), pp. 275–312. See also Horacio de la Costa, S. J., *Readings in Philippine History* (Makati City, Philippines: Bookmark, 1992), pages 172–85.
9. See Marcos, *Tadhana*, Vol. 2, Part III, pp. 338–43.
10. Lotilla, ed., *Philippine National Territory*, pp. 16-19.
11. De la Costa, *Readings in Philippine History*, pp. 183–85.
12. Lotilla, ed., *Philippine National Territory*, pp. 23–25.
13. Translation from the Malay in Arabic script by Professor Harold C. Conklin, 1946, as compiled in *The Philippine Claim to a Portion of North Borneo: Materials and Documents* (Quezon City, Philippines: Institute of International Legal Studies, University of the Philippines Law Center, 2003), p. 10.

14. De la Costa, *Readings in Philippine History*, p. 185.
15. The Bates Treaty is discussed in Peter Gordon Gowing, *Mandate in Moroland: The American Government of Muslim Filipinos 1899–1920* (Quezon City, Philippines: Philippine Center for Advanced Studies, University of the Philippines, 1977), pp. 31–37. The text of the treaty is in Appendix B of the book, pp. 348–49.
16. Ibid., pp. 32–33. Gowing uses the term "Moro" to refer to a Muslim Filipino, as did the Spaniards and the Americans and as the Muslim Filipinos themselves have done to this day.
17. Ibid., pp. 73–75.
18. Ibid., pp. 117–22.
19. The English translation of Sultan Jamalul Kiram II's letter to Governor-General Luke E. Wright is excerpted as Appendix C in Gowing, ibid., pp. 350–51.
20. See Gowing, ibid., pp. 284–87. The Carpenter Agreement is reproduced as Appendix D, pp. 352–53.
21. Ibid., pp. 336–44.
22. Lotilla, ed., *Philippine National Territory*, pp. 134–36.
23. Ibid., pp. 137–40.
24. Ibid., p. 418.
25. Ibid., p. 562.
26. Ibid., p. 569.
27. Gowing, *Mandate in Moroland*, pp. 204–207.
28. Lotilla, ed., *Philippine National Territory*, p. 168.
29. See Chapter 6.
30. Lotilla, ed., *Philippine National Territory*, pp. 148–56.
31. Ibid., pp. 157–66.
32. <http://www.chanrobles.com/1935constitutionofthephilippines.htm#1935%20 Constitution%20of%20the% 20Republic%20of%20the%20Philippines>.
33. <http://www.chanrobles.com/1899constitutionofthephilippines.htm>.
34. *Philippine Daily Inquirer*, 25 March 2008.
35. *Philippine Daily Inquirer*, 3 February 2009.
36. Lotilla, ed., *Philippine National Territory*, p. 146.
37. Ibid., p. 276.
38. Ibid., p. 274.

3

THE TERRITORY OF AN INDEPENDENT NATION

After the Philippines gained its independence from the United States on 4 July 1946, it continued to live under the 1935 Constitution, with its definition of the national territory. It did so until the promulgation by President Ferdinand E. Marcos of a new Constitution in January 1973.

THE 1973 PHILIPPINE CONSTITUTION

A Constitutional Convention, with over 300 members, had been drafting the new Constitution, since June 1971, when Marcos declared martial law in September 1972. The Convention continued working under martial law conditions. The final text was ratified in a nationwide plebiscite in January 1973. Like the 1935 Constitution, the 1973 document went out of its way to define the national territory. Article 1 of the 1973 Constitution had this to say about the subject:

> The national territory comprises the Philippine archipelago, with all the islands and waters embraced therein, and all the other territories belonging to the Philippines by historic right or legal title, including the territorial sea, the air space, the subsoil, the sea-bed, the insular shelves, and the submarine areas over which the Philippines has sovereignty or jurisdiction. The waters around, between, and connecting the islands of the archipelago, irrespective of their breadth and dimensions, form part of the internal waters of the Philippines.[1]

As in 1934, the 1971–72 Constitutional Convention debated the need to define the national territory in the new Constitution. Led by E. Voltaire

Garcia II, some of the delegates argued against the inclusion of such a definition. One of the grounds for the argument was that a definition would preclude the country from pursuing later territorial claims. Delegates also pointed out that questions of territory should be governed by international, rather than municipal, law. Related to this argument was the proposition that the actual exercise of authority over territory was a stronger basis for a claim than a unilateral declaration, which, in any case, was not binding on other nations. Moreover, basing territorial positions on treaties between colonial powers, as the original text of the proposed provision did, would only serve to remind Filipinos of their colonial past.

Other delegates asserted that a provision defining the national territory would serve notice to the world of the country's territorial jurisdiction and reaffirm its sovereignty over its internal waters and territorial sea. Some expressed the concern that references to future territorial claims as an argument for omitting a definition of the national territory would seem like an endorsement of imperialism. They also argued that the national territory needed to be defined in order to ensure that the national wealth was protected, security ensured, and national consciousness promoted.

In the end, the Convention rejected the amendment calling for deletion, 25–141, and approved, 177–14, the inclusion of the article on the national territory in the new Constitution. Unlike the 1935 Constitution, however, the 1973 document made no reference to the Treaty of Paris or to other international agreements pertaining to the Philippines' national territory. Rather, it referred more generally — and more flexibly — to "all the other territories belonging to the Philippines by historic right or legal title", but more specifically including the territorial sea, the air space, etc. The quoted phrase was meant to cover the Philippines' claim to Sabah and other, future claims to territory, including those over which the country was not exercising sovereignty at the time. As some delegates had proposed, the new Constitution contained no explicit references to pre-independence treaties and legislation in order to avoid invoking agreements concluded between colonial powers. Nevertheless, Eduardo Quintero, chairman of the Convention's Committee on National Territory, stated in response to a question from a colleague, that the phrase "historic right or legal title" encompassed such treaties and legislative acts.

Significantly, the territorial definition in the 1973 Constitution referred to the "Philippine archipelago, with all the islands and waters embraced therein", thereby asserting the archipelagic principle that the Philippines had been espousing internationally. The 1935 Constitution had merely defined Philippine territory in terms of what had been encompassed under treaties between the United States and Spain and between the United States and the United Kingdom.

Again like the 1935 Constitution, and also like the 1987 Constitution, the 1973 charter was a rarity in that it included a definition of the national territory. The Singapore, Thai and Vietnamese constitutions carry no provisions on those countries' territories. Neither did the revolutionary Philippine Constitution adopted at Malolos, north of Manila, in 1899. The current territory of Laos is the result of the Siamese-French agreement of 1907 and is not provided for in that country's constitution. Article 25A of the 1945 Indonesian Constitution merely states, "The Unitary State of the Republic of Indonesia is an archipelagic state, the boundaries and rights of whose territory shall be established by law." Indonesia has been seeking to consolidate its territory and maritime jurisdiction by negotiating agreements delimiting its land and maritime boundaries with neighbouring states, including with the Philippines.

Article 1 of the 1957 Malaysian Constitution declares:

> 2. The States of the Federation shall be Johore, Kedah, Kelantan, Malacca, Negri Sembilan, Pahang, Penang, Perak, Perlis, Sabah, Sarawak, Selangor and Trengganu.

> 3. Subject to Clause (4), the territories of each of the States mentioned in Clause (2) are the territories comprised therein immediately before Malaysia Day.

However, it refrains from defining the metes and bounds of those territories.

The constitution of a Southeast Asian state other than the Philippines that comes closest to defining its national territory is that of Cambodia. Article 2 of the 1993 Cambodian Constitution provides, "The territorial integrity of the Kingdom of Cambodia may absolutely not be violated within its borders as defined in the 1/100,000 scale map made between the years 1933-1953 and internationally recognized between the years 1963–1969."

In Northeast Asia, the constitution of neither Japan nor China has a provision on the national territory. Japan's current territorial boundaries were fixed by the San Francisco Treaty of 1951 (Treaty of Peace with Japan). In some cases, China has simply insisted on its claims in territorial disputes with neighbours and has refused to negotiate over them — the Paracels and the Spratlys in the South China Sea and the Diaoyu islands, which are disputed with Japan (which calls the islands the Senkakus). Beijing brooks no contestation over Taiwan or Tibet. On the other hand, it has settled boundary disputes with most other neighbours, including Burma, Nepal, North Korea, Russia, Mongolia, Vietnam (on land and in the Gulf of Tonkin, but not in the Paracels or the Spratlys in the South China Sea), Pakistan and Afghanistan. It has had long drawn-out discussions with India on their common border. China has legislated baselines off its southeastern coast and around the Paracels. However, there is no single document, much less a constitutional provision, that codifies the definition of Chinese territory as a whole.

The 1935 Philippine Constitution, with its definition of Philippine territory, had to conform to the Tydings-McDuffie Act. However, the U.S. Constitution itself does not define the country's territory (or contain any provisions for the acquisition or relinquishment of territory). Indeed, in the Louisiana Purchase of 1803, long after the adoption of its Constitution, the United States bought from France more than 23 per cent of the land area of what is now the United States. The purchase was for US$15 million, including the assumption of claims of American citizens against France. Texas joined the United States in 1845 after a brief period of independence from Mexico. As part of the settlement of the Mexican-American War under the Treaty of Guadalupe Hidalgo of 1848, Mexico ceded to the United States what are now California, Nevada, Utah and Arizona and parts of what are now Wyoming, Colorado and New Mexico. Russia sold Alaska to the United States in 1867 for US$7.2 million or about five cents per hectare.

As stated in Chapter 2 of this book, the 1898 Treaty of Paris found it necessary to specify the imaginary lines encompassing the islands that Spain was ceding to the United States in order to make clear exactly what was being ceded. This was subsequently referred to in the 1935 Constitution, but not explicitly in the succeeding ones. In any case, as some have claimed, the inclusion of a provision on the national territory in the 1935 Constitution was at least partly motivated by the desire to make sure that the extent of Philippine territory remained intact upon the attainment of independence and thereafter and to forestall any efforts to separate Mindanao and Sulu, or any attempts by those islands to secede, from the rest of the country.

THE BASELINES AND THE SABAH CLAIM

By the time of the promulgation of the 1973 Constitution, the Philippines had enacted a law, in 1961, "to Define the Baselines of the Territorial Sea of the Philippines". That law proclaimed in its preamble that "all the waters around, between and connecting the various islands of the Philippine archipelago, irrespective of their width or dimensions, ..." form "part of the inland or internal waters of the Philippines" and that "all the waters beyond the outermost islands of the archipelago but within the limits of the boundaries set forth" in the 1898 Treaty of Paris, the 1900 U.S.-Spain treaty, and the U.S.-U.K. convention of 1930 "comprise the territorial sea of the Philippines".[2] In introducing this piece of legislation in the twenty-four-member Philippine Senate, Senator Arturo Tolentino, head of the Philippine delegation to all three UN conferences on the law of the sea, explained that the bill was making a necessary distinction between internal waters and the territorial sea. According to Tolentino, international law confers on the state sovereignty over internal waters to the same extent as over its land territory, and over bodies of water like rivers and lakes, while it allows vessels of other states the right of "innocent passage" through the territorial sea. It had been found necessary to draw baselines around the Philippine archipelago so as to prevent others from claiming the right of "innocent passage" in what the Philippines insisted were its internal waters and to ensure that each Philippine island was not considered as generating its own territorial sea, whose breadth was in dispute at the time and would be agreed upon only in the 1982 UNCLOS. In his sponsorship speech, Tolentino explained that it was necessary to make the adjustments because of what he called "developments" in the March 1960 conference on the law of the sea in Geneva and, adding cryptically, in order to be "of utility" to the Philippine delegation then negotiating the treaty of commerce and navigation with Japan.[3]

Seven years later, in 1968, Senator Tolentino introduced a bill in the Senate seeking to adjust the baselines "to correct typographical errors". He explained that the bill would retain the provision in the old baselines act that declared, "All waters within the baselines provided for in Section one hereof are considered inland or internal waters of the Philippines."[4]

During the period of amendment, Senator Juan Liwag proposed the insertion of a provision that would further assert the Philippines' claim to parts of North Borneo in terms of the delineation of baselines around Sabah. As eventually enacted, the provision read, "The definition of the baselines of the territorial sea of the Philippine Archipelago as provided in this Act is without prejudice to the delineation of the baselines around the territory of Sabah, situated in North Borneo, over which the Republic of the Philippines has acquired dominion and sovereignty." Tolentino, as principal sponsor of the bill, readily accepted the amendment.

In the House of Representatives, Carmelo Z. Barbero proposed a similar amendment to the counterpart bill. The principal sponsor of the House bill, Frisco San Juan, at first hesitated to accept it, expressing his concern that other countries' objections to the proposed reservation might jeopardize the Philippines' other objectives at the international conferences on the law of the sea, mainly the world's acceptance of the archipelagic concept and its recognition of the waters between islands as internal. In the end, under apparent pressure from representatives from Mindanao and Sulu, he relented, and the bill, with its amendment, was approved by the House without a dissenting vote.[5]

After these debates, the bill was approved in September 1968. All this was happening as the Philippines-Malaysia dispute over Sabah heated up once again, with diplomatic relations between the two countries suspended as a direct consequence of the Jabidah Massacre of March 1968, as well as of the passage of the 1968 baselines act with its Sabah-related amendment.[6]

THE 1987 CONSTITUTION

After a popular uprising in support of a significant faction of the Philippine military overthrew Marcos on 25 February 1986, the 1973 Constitution was abrogated. As a temporary measure, the new President, Corazon C. Aquino, promulgated, by a Presidential Proclamation on 25 March, the so-called "Freedom Constitution", which kept unchanged, along with four other articles, Article I of the 1973 Constitution, that on the national territory. President Aquino then appointed a fifty-member Constitutional Commission to work on a new, permanent constitution. The document, completed and approved without a dissenting vote in October 1986 (Commissioner Lino Brocka, the famed film director, had resigned his membership) and ratified in a popular plebiscite in February 1987, restored many of the provisions of the 1935 Constitution. On the national territory, Article I of the 1987 Constitution retains for the most part the corresponding article of the 1973 Constitution, but, significantly, replaces "all the other territories belonging to the Philippines by historic right or legal title" (which was also the formulation in the original draft of Article I of the 1987 Constitution) with "all other territories over which the Philippines has sovereignty or jurisdiction". The change was made, on the proposal of Jesuit lawyer Joaquin Bernas, S. J., in order, as Father Bernas explained it, to exclude any phrase that could be interpreted as asserting the Philippine claim to Sabah in the Philippine Constitution and thus result in the "unnecessary" exacerbation of Philippine-Malaysian animosity over the Sabah issue.

Thus, the 1987 Constitution, which remains in force, states:

> The national territory comprises the Philippine archipelago, with all the islands and waters embraced therein, and all other territories over which the Philippines has sovereignty or jurisdiction, consisting of its terrestrial, fluvial

and aerial domains, including its territorial sea, the seabed, the subsoil, the insular shelves, and other submarine areas. The waters around, between, and connecting the islands of the archipelago, regardless of their breadth and dimensions, form part of the internal waters of the Philippines.[7]

To Raphael Perpetuo Lotilla, a leading Philippine authority on maritime law, this change is significant. He writes:

> The deletion from the 1987 Constitution of explicit references in the 1935 Constitution to the different treaties drawing lines around the Philippine archipelago, and in the 1973 Constitution to "territories belonging to the Philippines by historic right and legal title", helps support the view that the LOS Convention does not contravene the Constitution on the extent of the Philippines' territorial waters. While the 1987 Constitution contains the phrase "and all other territories over which the Philippines has sovereignty or jurisdiction", which some interpret as embodying the provisions appearing in the 1935 and 1973 Constitutions, the present phraseology no longer provides as strong a support for the claim to historic waters as those found in the 1935 and 1973 Constitutions.[8]

From another perspective, Lotilla's view and those of others evidently maintain that the provisions on the national territory in the 1987 Constitution are not inconsistent with the UNCLOS, just as the Philippines' ratification of the UNCLOS did not violate the Constitution. Some governments dispute this. At the same time, it may be asked whether the omission of "by historic right and legal title" weakens the Philippine claim to Sabah, as Senator Juan Ponce Enrile implies in his website.[9]

In fact, much of the debate in the Constitutional Commission over the Bernas amendment, and over the inclusion in the new Constitution of a provision on the national territory at all, revolved around the Sabah issue. The amendment, which replaced "belonging to the Philippines by historic right or legal title" with "over which the Philippines has sovereignty or jurisdiction", was eventually approved, 39–4. Many of those who voted in favour of the amendment did so upon the assurance of Father Bernas that the new formulation would neither assert the Philippine claim to Sabah nor imply its abandonment, but rather "prescind" from the issue.

Father Bernas actually preferred not to have a provision on the national territory at all, supporting René Sarmiento's proposal for its deletion, a proposal also backed by José B. Laurel, Jr. Sarmiento argued that the provision's omission would not have any effect on the country's sovereignty over any part of its territory, that its inclusion would not legitimize any territorial claim that was not based on evidence or legal right, and that its deletion would help avoid straining relations with other countries. Father Bernas pointed out that the Constitution had the nature of "municipal law" and was thus not binding on other nations, while Laurel noted that the omission of the provision would give the government more flexibility in the future.

On the other hand, those who favoured the inclusion of the article on the national territory recalled that such an article had been inserted in previous Philippine constitutions in order to maintain the unity of the Philippines' territory. They also pointed out that the corresponding article in the 1973 Constitution affirmed the archipelagic principle and the concept of internal waters that the Philippines had been espousing and that the phrase "historic right or legal title" had been meant to assert the claim to Sabah. To omit the national territory provision from the new constitution would imply a retreat from these positions. One commissioner, Ambrosio Padilla, noted that, while the Philippine Constitution had the nature of "municipal law" that was not binding on others, states did accord one another "respect and courtesy". Others maintained that the invocation, explicit in the 1935 Constitution and implicit in the 1973 Constitution, of the Treaty of Paris and other international covenants defining Philippine territory was internationally binding.

By the time the 1987 Constitution entered into force, the Philippines had signed the UNCLOS, in 1982, and had ratified it, in 1984. Manila had enacted legislation in anticipation of the convention's entry into force, adjusting the country's baselines in 1968 and declaring its exclusive economic zone as projected from those baselines in 1978. It had also further formalized, by legislation enacted in 1978, its claim to a large "area" of the South China Sea and to the islands and other land features within the ambit of its claim, "including the seabed, subsoil, continental margin and air space", declaring Kalayaan, as the area was to be called, a municipality of the province of Palawan.

THE QUESTION OF INTERNAL WATERS

The insistence in the current Philippine Constitution, which entered into force after the country signed and ratified the UNCLOS, that the "waters around, between, and connecting the islands of the archipelago, *regardless of their breadth and dimensions* (italics mine), form part of the internal waters of the Philippines" seems to be inconsistent with Articles 7 and 47 of the UNCLOS. Those articles quite precisely lay down the conditions under which an archipelagic state may draw its baselines and those under which a body of water within such baselines may be considered as internal.

Article 7 provides, among other things, that the "drawing of straight baselines must not depart to any appreciable extent from the general direction of the coast, and the sea areas lying within the lines must be sufficiently closely linked to the land domain to be subject to the regime of internal waters". Article 47 states in part:

1. An archipelagic State may draw straight archipelagic baselines joining the outermost points of the outermost islands and drying reefs of the archipelago provided that within such baselines are included the main islands and an area in which the ratio of the area of the water to the area of the land ... is between 1 to 1 and 9 to 1.

2. The length of such baselines shall not exceed 100 nautical miles, except that up to 3 per cent of the total number of baselines enclosing any archipelago may exceed that length, up to a maximum length of 125 nautical miles.

3. The drawing of such baselines shall not depart to any appreciable extent from the general configuration of the archipelago.[10]

In order to get around this apparent contradiction, some Philippine officials and scholars have proposed that, in the case of bodies of water that do not strictly satisfy UNCLOS requirements, the phrase "internal waters", as used in the Constitution, be applied and interpreted not necessarily as "internal waters" in the UNCLOS sense but rather as "archipelagic waters" or some other regime consistent with the UNCLOS. Lotilla asserts, "In the absence of a clear intent on the part of the framers of the 1987 Constitution to override the provisions of the Convention ..., it can be suggested that the terms 'internal' and 'archipelagic' are interchangeable in the context of the Philippine Constitution.... The Constitution and the LOS Convention can be made compatible since the latter recognizes that the archipelagic State's sovereignty extends over archipelagic waters subject to particular provisions of the Convention."[11] Indeed, as Lotilla recalls, the head of the Philippine delegation, Arturo Tolentino, upon signing the UNCLOS in December 1982, declared, among other things, that the "concept of archipelagic waters is similar to the concept of internal waters under the Constitution of the Philippines".

After the Philippines ratified the UNCLOS in 1984, several UN members rejected the 1982 Philippine declaration, which was reaffirmed upon ratification. The Byelorussian Soviet Socialist Republic (then part of the Soviet Union and now Belarus), Czechoslovakia (since then split into the Czech Republic and Slovakia), the Union of Soviet Socialist Republics (to which the Russian Federation is the successor-state), the Ukranian Soviet Socialist Republic (then part of the Soviet Union and now Ukraine), and Australia charged that the Philippine declaration amounted to reservations disallowed by Articles 309 and 310 of the UNCLOS and accused the Philippines of giving primacy to its domestic laws over the convention. Some of them objected to the Philippines' conflation of archipelagic and internal waters. China and Vietnam protested against the Philippine assertion of its claim to parts of the South China Sea, to which the two countries had conflicting claims. The United States, too, rejected the primacy that the Philippines seemed to give to its domestic law over the rights and obligations conferred by the UNCLOS or other "customary and conventional" international law. The United States specifically objected to the 1973 Philippine Constitution's claim to "internal waters", asserting that "the concept of internal waters differs significantly from the concept of archipelagic waters" and explaining how. Most significantly, it stressed that neither the United States nor the Philippines as its successor-state enjoyed under bilateral treaties, including the Philippines-U.S. Mutual Defence Treaty, more rights in the waters surrounding the Philippines than those recognized "in customary international law".

In response to the Australian objection, the Philippines gave assurances that Manila would "abide by the provisions of the said Convention". Specifically, the Philippines declared that its government "intends to harmonize its domestic legislation with the provisions of the Convention" and that the "necessary steps are being undertaken to enact legislation dealing with archipelagic sea lanes passage and the exercise of Philippine sovereign rights over archipelagic waters, in accordance with the Convention".

DECISIONS MUST BE MADE

The debate persists on the maritime regime governing the waters between the baselines and the Treaty of Paris limits. The March 2009 baselines act amends the 1961 law as amended in 1968. It adjusts the archipelago's baselines, but does not explicitly do away with the references in the preamble of the 1961 law to the 1898 Treaty of Paris, the 1900 U.S.-Spain agreement and the U.S.-U.K. Convention of 1930. Neither did the 1968 law. The 1961 preamble declares that "all the waters within the limits set forth in the above-mentioned treaties have always been regarded (not saying by whom) as part of the territory of the Philippine Islands" and that "all the waters beyond the outermost islands of the archipelago but within the limits of the boundaries set forth in the aforementioned treaties comprise the territorial sea of the Philippines". However, the new law states, "The provisions of Republic Act

No. 3046, as amended by Republic Act No. 5446, and all other laws, decrees, executive orders, rules and issuances inconsistent with this Act are hereby amended or modified accordingly." At the same time, in its title, it identifies "to define the archipelagic baselines of the Philippines" as one of its objectives. Section 1 refers to "the baselines of the Philippine archipelago". The new act thus implicitly acknowledges that the country is not only an archipelago in the geographic sense but an archipelagic state as defined in the UNCLOS.[12] This seems to be a significant change from the superseded law, which defined "the Baselines of the Territorial Sea of the Philippines". It could be argued that, by terming the baselines as "archipelagic", the Philippines, by law, now considers itself as an archipelagic state. Indeed, in the executive summary of the "partial submission" that it made in April 2009 to the UN Commission on the Limits of the Continental Shelf, the Philippines refers to itself as an "archipelagic State".

Accordingly, the Philippine government has started to undertake consultations on the designation of archipelagic sea lanes in accordance with Article 53 of the UNCLOS, which allows archipelagic states to designate sea lanes and air routes "suitable for the continuous and expeditious passage of foreign ships and aircraft through or over its archipelagic waters and the adjacent territorial sea".

Having passed the Philippine Congress on 17 February 2009, the baselines bill was signed into law by President Gloria Macapagal-Arroyo on 10 March 2009. According to the UN, the Philippine Government deposited its text with the Secretary-General on 1 April 2009.[13] A week later, it made its "partial submission" of data and information on the outer limits of its claimed continental shelf to the UN Commission on the Limits of the Continental Shelf. Article 76 of the UNCLOS allows a state to claim a continental shelf beyond a breadth of 200 nautical miles from its baselines but not to exceed 350 nautical miles. It lays down the procedures for making such submissions to the UN Commission, which is to make its recommendations to the coastal state. The Philippines made its submission on 8 April 2009, a little over a month before the 13 May 2009 deadline — for the Philippines — for such submissions. The Philippine submission covers only Benham Rise, off the northeastern coast of Luzon, as an area "not subject to any maritime boundary disputes, claims, or controversies" and reserves the right to make other submissions in the future. This is why it is called a "partial submission". The new law makes no explicit reference to any provision of the Philippine Constitution or the Treaty of Paris or other international agreements that relate to the country's national territory or maritime regime.[14]

However, on the same day that the government made its "partial submission", two University of the Philippines law professors, Merlin Magallona and Harry Roque, a number of law students in the university, and a member of the House of Representatives, Risa Hontiveros, filed a petition asking the Supreme Court to order the government to refrain from implementing the new baselines law, specifically from submitting it to the UN, as the law called for. The petition charged that the law's implementation would "result in palpable violations of the Constitution" and that its submission to the UN would "forever close the door to any Philippine efforts to obtain the acceptance of the international community of our Constitutionally-defined national territory" and "immediately bind the Philippines to the UNCLOS III regime, leading to the dismemberment of the Philippine national territory as defined in the 1987 Constitution".[15]

The Supreme Court on 7 April ordered the government to respond to the petition within ten days. By that time, the government had deposited the new baselines law with the UN in accordance with Article 47 of the UNCLOS. The day after the Supreme Court's order, the government made its submission to the UN Commission in New York. Thus, the government responded that these acts had rendered moot the petition before the Supreme Court.

The declaration in the March 2009 baselines act of a "regime of islands" with respect to the land features in the South China Sea that Manila claims and to Scarborough Shoal, which it also claims, seems to clarify in some measure the nature and extent of those claims and harmonise them with the UNCLOS. As expected, that declaration, as well as the claims in general, has been challenged by both Beijing and Hanoi.

On the basis of the new baselines law alone, the Philippines retains the option of drawing baselines around the Kalayaan islands and/or Scarborough Shoal and its related land features. However, by declaring a regime of islands for them pursuant to Article 121 of the UNCLOS, the Philippines seems to have inched its way towards consistency with the UNCLOS in so far as its South China Sea claims are concerned.

The Philippine claim to Sabah, of course, has its implications for the maritime regime. Not only did the Philippine legislature use the 1968 amendment to the baselines act to re-assert the claim. The Philippine-Malaysian dispute has halted the scope of the negotiations between the Philippines and Indonesia on the delimitation of their maritime boundary at the point where the boundary would intersect the limits of Sabah waters. It has also prevented Philippine-Malaysian cooperation on fisheries and other matters in waters that are in dispute between them and made anti-crime coordination in the area more difficult.

The Philippines as a sovereign nation has to make up its official mind about these and a number of other issues. These are raised in subsequent chapters and summarized in the concluding one.

Notes

1. <http://www.chanrobles.com/1973constitutionofthephilippines.htm>.
2. Raphael Perpetuo M. Lotilla, ed., *The Philippine National Territory: A Collection of Related Documents* (Diliman, Quezon City: Institute of International Legal Studies, University of the Philippines Law Center, and Manila: Foreign Service Institute, Department of Foreign Affairs, 1995), p. 276.
3. Ibid., p. 281 et seq.
4. Ibid., p. 373.
5. Ibid., p. 375 et seq.
6. See Chapter 4.
7. <http://www.chanrobles.com/article1.htm>.
8. Raphael Perpetuo M. Lotilla, "Philippine Implementation of the UNCLOS: Issues, Problems, and Prospects", in *Proceedings and Selected Papers Presented at the Phuket and Chiangmai SEAPOL Workshops (1989 and 1991)* (Bangkok: South-East Asian Programme in Ocean Law, Policy and Management, 1992), p. 20.
9. <http://www.jpenrile.com/advocacies/article.asp?advocacy=reforms&folder=spe ech&article=007.
10. <http://www.un.org/Depts/los/convention_agreements/texts/unclos/closindx. htm>, Article 47.
11. Lotilla, "Philippine Implementation of the UNCLOS", p. 18.
12. <http://www.lawphil.net/statutes/repacts/ra2009/ra_9522_2009.html>.
13. <http://www.un.org/Depts/los/LEGISLATIONANDTREATIES/PDFFILES/ mzn_s/mzn69.pdf>.
14 The executive summary of the Philippine submission is in <http://www.un.org/ Depts/los/clcs_new/ submissions_files/ phl22_09/phl_esummary.pdf>.
15. <http://verafiles.org/docs/manifestmotionapril2.pdf>.

4

THE CLAIM TO SABAH

On 22 January 1878, Sultan Jamalul Alam of Sulu executed a document, "with the expressed desire of all Datus in common agreement", leasing (according to the English translation from the Malay in Arabic script used by the Philippines, but "grant and cede" according to the translation employed by the British) "to Gustavus Baron de Overbeck of Hong Kong, and to Alfred Dent ... of London, ... as representatives of a British Company, together with their heirs, associates, successors and assigns forever and until the end of time, all rights and powers which we possess over all territories and lands tributary to us on the mainland of the Island of Borneo, ... together with all the islands which lie within nine miles of the coast", defining the metes and bounds of the territory in question in terms of natural features and administrative subdivisions. In return, Overbeck and Dent were to pay the Sultan and "his heirs or successors" five thousand Malayan dollars (increased in 1903 to five thousand three hundred), "to be paid each and every year". W. H. Treacher, Britain's Acting Consul General in Borneo, witnessed the Sultan's seal and signature on the document.[1]

Six months later, Carlos Martínez, the Spanish Colonel-General (Governor) of Sulu, wrote to Baron de Overbeck informing him that Sultan Jamalul Alam of Sulu had on the same day, 22 July 1878, communicated in writing to the Spanish authorities his decision "to cancel the contract for lease of Sandakan and the rest" on account of Overbeck's failure "to fulfill the contract of lease", as well as the fact that "the Crown of Spain has possession of all the territory of this Sultanate". In his reply to the Governor of Sulu, Overbeck rejected the contract's cancellation. In a 2 July letter to the "Governor Captain-General of the Philippines", the Sultan had claimed that he had been forced to sign the contract of lease — or cession — upon Overbeck's threat that the Captain-General would come, presumably with his forces, and "destroy everything".

In December 1878, Dent and Overbeck recounted the grant of Borneo territories by the Sultan of Sulu and four previous grants by the Sultan of Brunei to a private association formed by Dent "for the purpose of acquiring territorial grants in North Borneo and developing its resources". They then sought from the British foreign minister a charter of incorporation and regulation for a proposed company that would have extra-territorial jurisdiction over British subjects, British protection, and support by the British government with respect to foreign states. In November 1881, the British government granted the requested charter to the British North Borneo Company. Under the charter, the new company was to take over from the British North Borneo Provisional Association its interests in and powers over territories and property, including specifically those in Borneo and nearby islands. At the same time, the new company would "fulfill the promises of payment and other promises therein made, subject to any subsequent agreement affecting those promises". Monopoly on trade was expressly prohibited.

According to a letter of Earl Granville, the British foreign minister at the time, to the British minister in Madrid, dated 7 January 1882, Spain, as well as The Netherlands, protested against Britain's grant of a charter to the British North Borneo Company. Earl Granville asserted that neither Britain nor Germany had recognized Spain's claim to sovereignty over Sulu and its dependencies because of Spain's failure to maintain control over those territories. By a treaty between Spain and the Sultan of Sulu, signed on 22 July 1878, the Sultan had, according to the Spaniards, recognized Spanish sovereignty over Sulu and its tributaries on the northeastern coast of Borneo. The British, however, continued to object to Spanish claims "to sovereignty over any part of Borneo". Earl Granville declared that "there was no question of the annexation of North Borneo by Great Britain, or of the establishment of the British Protectorate there". Going on, he pointed out that "the Crown in the present case assumes no dominion or sovereignty over the territories occupied by the Company ... and recognizes the grants of territory and the powers of government made and delegated by the Sultans in whom sovereignty remains vested".

BRITISH MOVES AND PHILIPPINE ARGUMENTS

Nevertheless, on 12 May 1888, Great Britain did establish a protectorate over "the State of North Borneo". On 26 June 1946, eight days before the Philippines regained her independence, the British Crown concluded with the British North Borneo Company an agreement under which it took "full sovereign rights over, and title to, the territory of the State of North Borneo". The Crown also assumed all the assets and liabilities of the company. In turn, it undertook to pay the company a sum to be determined by arbitration. On 10 July 1946, six days after the resumption of Philippine independence, the North Borneo Cession Order in Council, 1946, declared that, effective on 15 July 1946, the "State of North Borneo shall be annexed to and shall form part of His Majesty's dominions and shall be called, together with the Settlement of Labuan and its dependencies, the Colony of North Borneo".

In December 1946, H. Otley Beyer, the eminent former head of the Department of Anthropology at the University of the Philippines, raised questions about the legality of the instrument by which Sultan Jamalul Alam had leased — or ceded — "the territories allegedly owned by him in northern Borneo" in January 1878. In a memorandum accompanying the English translation by his assistant, Harold G. Conklin, of the instrument's Malay text, Beyer noted that, unlike other documents of this nature, it bore only the signature and seal of Jamalul Alam and was not witnessed or signed by any other member of the Ruma Bechara (state council). He pointed out that, unlike the Malay sultanates, the Sulu Sultanate was governed collectively by the Sultan and the Ruma Bechara, which consisted of datus and other powerful chiefs. The Sultan, Beyer argued, could not by himself have legally alienated such a large tract of land that belonged not to him personally but to the Sultanate as a whole.

Beyer was of the view that the agreement that Frank Carpenter, the first Governor of the (American civilian) Department of Mindanao and Sulu, had signed with the Sultan of Sulu in March 1915 did not abolish the Sulu Sultanate. Under the "memorandum agreement", the Sultan of Sulu recognized the sovereignty of the United States "in Mindanao and Sulu" (but not in North Borneo).

Beyer quoted Carpenter as telling the Director of Non-Christian Tribes in the Philippines in a letter dated May 1920 that "the termination of the temporal sovereignty of the Sultanate of Sulu within American territory is understood to be wholly without prejudice or effect as to the temporal sovereignty and ecclesiastical authority of the Sultanate beyond the jurisdiction of the United States Government, especially with reference to the portion of the Island of Borneo which as a dependency of the Sultanate of Sulu is understood to be held under lease by the chartered company which is known as the 'British North Borneo Government'" (sic).

Beyer also quoted Dent as telling the Royal Colonial Institute in May 1885:

> As to the charter, some friends of the enterprise seem to believe that the enormous powers we hold were given by Her Majesty the Queen. It is not so at all. All our powers were derived entirely from the Sultans of Brunei and Sulu, and what the British government did was simply to incorporate us by Royal Charter....

In September 1946, F. B. Harrison, former American Governor-General of the Philippines and then adviser to the President of an independent Philippines, urged the Philippine Government to protest Great Britain's proclamation of North Borneo as a British Crown Colony "in derogation of the rights of the Sultanate of Sulu". In a later memorandum, to Vice-President Elpidio Quirino, concurrently Secretary of Foreign Affairs, dated February 1947, Harrison, like Beyer before him, forwarded Conklin's English translation of the January 1878 Malay-language document, which said that the Sultan of Sulu had granted to Overbeck and Dent "a permanent lease covering his lands and territories on the island of Borneo". The document, according to Harrison, had been obtained by the U.S. Department of State from the British government and discovered by a Philippine official.

Meanwhile, in June 1936, the Sultan of Sulu, Jamalul Kiram II, had died childless. Ruling on a civil suit filed by proprietary claimants, Chief Justice C. F. C. Macaskie of the High Court of North Borneo designated the following as heirs of the deceased Sultan, with their corresponding shares of the "cession money" (the term rendered in the Maxwell-Gibson translation used by Justice Macaskie):

Dayang Dayang Haji Piandao	3/8
Putli Tarhata Kiram	3/16
Putli Sakinurin Kiram	3/16
Mora Napsa	1/24
Esmail Kiram	1/24
Punjungan Kiram	1/24
Mariam Kiram	1/24
Rada Kiram	1/24
Putli Jahara Kiram	1/24

All the nine persons named have since died, the last one being Putli Sakinurin, in November 1987. Ulka Ulama, a lawyer, has for years received the 5,300 Malaysian ringgit from the Malaysian government on behalf of the heirs of most of these heirs. In the 2000s, the Malaysian embassy in Manila has been remitting to Ulama cheques of more than 70 thousand Philippine pesos every year. Some of the heirs have impugned the legitimacy of others. At the same time, a number of personalities have emerged from the woodwork claiming somehow to be heirs and thus hoping for at least parts of an anticipated compensatory lump-sum from the Malaysians.

Raul S. Manglapus was an eloquent and far-seeing Filipino politician, Undersecretary of Foreign Affairs under President Ramón Magsaysay, twice a Senator, and President Corazon Aquino's Secretary of Foreign Affairs from 1987 to 1992. Putting on a British accent, he used to tell the story of how the British, during the Magsaysay administration (1953–57), had privately hinted that a sizeable influx of Filipino workers into Sabah could help the Philippines take the claimed territory. However, according to Manglapus, the Philippine Government imposed so many conditions on the employment of Filipinos that the scheme was abandoned.

On the other hand, the report of the committee on the national territory of the Constitutional Commission that produced the 1987 Philippine Constitution had this to say:

> Mr. (Blas) Ople (Ferdinand Marcos's Minister of Labor, member of the 1986 Constitutional Commission, Senator, and finally Secretary of Foreign Affairs under President Gloria Macapagal-Arroyo until his death in December 2003) also informed the Body that during the incumbency of President Magsaysay, British North Borneo, now known as Sabah, had wanted an assured yearly supply of 10,000 Filipino immigrant workers but it unilaterally backed out from the agreement after hearing reports of imminent Philippine claims over Sabah.[2]

In April 1950, the Philippine House of Representatives passed a resolution sponsored by then-Congressman Diosdado Macapagal and a number of others authorizing the government "to negotiate with the British Government or to take other suitable steps" for the restoration of the ownership of British North Borneo to the heirs of the Sultan of Sulu and the recognition of Philippine sovereignty over it.

On 25 November 1957, Sultan Esmail Kiram of Sulu declared the termination of the "lease" to Overbeck and Dent and the restoration of all the lands covered by that arrangement to the Sultanate of Sulu.[3] The Sultan stressed that the 1878 deed of Sultan Jamalul Alam had been one of lease and not of cession or sale and that "sovereignty and dominion ... over North Borneo" had remained with the Sultan of Sulu. Esmail Kiram, claiming to have the "consent and approval of the Ruma Bechara, ... ceded and transferred", on 24 April 1962, sovereignty and dominion over North Borneo to the Republic of the Philippines. The Philippine Government promptly — that is, the next day — accepted the transfer.[4]

THE CREATION OF MALAYSIA AND
THE PHILIPPINE RESPONSE

In May 1962, after the Philippine House of Representatives had urged the President "to take the necessary steps ... for the recovery of North Borneo", Great Britain warned the Philippine government that "Her Majesty's Government would be bound to resist any claim to part of North Borneo, whether advanced by the Philippine Government or by private persons in the Philippines". The British aide-mémoire continued, "Moreover, the Governments of the United Kingdom and Malaya welcomed in principle proposals for a new and independent Federation of Malaya (sic) which unite the present independent Federation of Malaya with North Borneo and Brunei, Sarawak and Singapore."[5]

It was the view at that time that North Borneo, Brunei and Sarawak were to be included in the new federation in order to offset, with people considered as *bumiputra* (Malay and other "indigenous" people), the overwhelmingly Chinese population that Singapore's inclusion would bring in. In his latest book, Nicholas Tarling, a New Zealand scholar, quotes the British Foreign Secretary, the Earl of Home, as saying in August 1961 that the Malayan leader, Tunku Abdul Rahman, was showing interest in "Greater Malaysia" on the basis of the idea that he could "absorb the Chinese population of Singapore by bringing in the Borneo Territories to redress the racial balance; at the same time this might forestall Indonesian ambitions in the area".[6] In a speech to a foreign journalists' association in May 1961 proposing a new Malaysia made up of Malaya, Sabah, Sarawak and Singapore, Tunku Abdul Rahman had explicitly stressed this point. J.A.C. Mackie of the Centre of Southeast Asian Studies at Monash University in Australia has written, "The central purpose behind the creation of Malaysia was to make possible the merger of Singapore and the Malayan Federation, without creating a Chinese majority which would have endangered the existing political primacy of the Malays in an enlarged state."[7]

It seems somewhat bizarre to recall now that Singapore was then considered not only as overwhelmingly Chinese by race but also as a potential communist threat, although that possibility was, at the time, considered seriously by all concerned. There was a similar apprehension pertaining to the large Chinese population on the Malayan peninsula. For a variety of reasons, Brunei

Darussalam eventually opted out of the proposed federation. Singapore separated from Malaysia in 1965.

In June 1962, the Philippines disputed the British position and proposed "conversations" between the Philippine and British governments.[8] After initial British reluctance, those "conversations" finally took place in London early in 1963.

The leader of the Philippine delegation, Vice President and Secretary of Foreign Affairs Emmanuel Peláez, gave a brief summary of the Philippine claim. He stressed that the British Crown could not have acquired sovereignty over North Borneo from the British North Borneo Company, since the latter, being a private company, did not have the capacity to acquire such sovereignty. Neither did Alfred Dent and Baron de Overbeck, who had applied for a Royal Charter on behalf of the British North Borneo Provisional Association, the predecessor of the British North Borneo Company, and other associates. In any case, Peláez recalled, the British government had disavowed assuming dominion or sovereignty over the territories that the company occupied in North Borneo or purporting to grant to the company "any powers of government" over them. He also affirmed the Philippine view that the deed that the Sultan of Sulu had executed in favour of Overbeck and Dent was one of lease and not of sale or cession. The Sultanate of Sulu retained dominion and sovereignty over its territories in North Borneo. Peláez then proposed a deferment of the formation of Malaysia in order to allow for both "a short-range solution to the question of North Borneo" and eventually a permanent "accommodation" among Indonesia, Malaya and the Philippines. For his part, another legal luminary on the Philippine delegation, Jovito Salonga, a member of the Philippine House of Representatives, repeated some of Peláez's arguments and added that, under the Carpenter Agreement of 1915, the Sultan of Sulu had given up his temporal authority in U.S. territory but not outside it, particularly not in North Borneo.[9]

In his book, Tarling, the New Zealand scholar, writes that the grant of a Royal Charter creating the British North Borneo Company "did not make North Borneo British". Among the "anomalies" that Tarling cites as having been created by the British moves was "a Company with ruling powers derived from the Sultans but constrained by a Royal Charter". He declares that North Borneo, Brunei and Sarawak "did not become British" by virtue of the protectorate agreements that Britain concluded with them in 1888.[10]

In his address to the UN General Assembly in October 1963, Salvador P. López, the Philippines' Acting Secretary of Foreign Affairs, recounted his country's view of the events leading to the proclamation of Malaysia. He recalled the summit meeting in Manila among the Philippines' Macapagal,

Indonesia's Sukarno and Malaya's Tunku Abdul Rahman from 30 July to 5 August to discuss their differences over the proposed formation of Malaysia. They approved the Manila Accord, which had been adopted by their foreign ministers — Peláez, Subandrio and Tun Abdul Razak. The summit laid down certain guidelines for the settlement of their dispute over Malaysia and established a consultative organization called MAPHILINDO (for Malaysia, the Philippines and Indonesia), with Indonesia, López said, willing to welcome Malaysia if it was "purged of its neo-colonialist taint" and the Philippines prepared to do so as long as Sabah's inclusion in the new federation would not prejudice its claim to the territory. The three leaders called on the UN Secretary-General to ascertain the wishes of the people of Sabah and Sarawak, before the formation of Malaysia, through a "fresh approach".

Philippine foreign ministers reiterated the Philippine arguments, in varying detail, at the UN General Assembly every year at least until 1970. Particular emphasis was placed on self-determination and the peaceful nature of the means with which the Philippines intended to pursue its claim to North Borneo. The Philippines stressed the legal character of the claim, which warranted its adjudication by the International Court of Justice. As the years went by, with Sabah becoming increasingly entrenched in Malaysia, recourse to the ICJ became the main objective of the Philippines' presentations at the General Assembly.[11]

The Manila Accord to which Peláez had referred had been adopted by the Indonesian, Malayan and Philippine foreign ministers at their meeting on 7–11 June and signed by their leaders on 31 July 1963. It said in part:

10. The Ministers reaffirmed their countries' adherence to the principle of self-determination for the peoples of non-self-governing territories. In this context, Indonesia and the Philippines stated that they would welcome the formation of Malaysia provided the support of the people of the Borneo territories is ascertained by an independent and impartial authority, the Secretary-General of the United Nations or his representative.

11. The Federation of Malaya expressed appreciation for this attitude of Indonesia and the Philippines and undertook to consult the British Government and the Governments of the Borneo territories with a view to inviting the Secretary-General of the United Nations or his representative to take the necessary steps in order to ascertain the wishes of the people of those territories,

12. The Philippines made it clear that its position on the inclusion of North Borneo in the Federation of Malaysia is subject to the final outcome of the Philippine claim to North Borneo. The Ministers took note of the

Philippine claim and the right of the Philippines to continue to pursue it in accordance with international law and the principle of the pacific settlement of disputes. They agreed that the inclusion of North Borneo in the Federation of Malaysia would not prejudice either the claim or any right thereunder. Moreover, in the context of their close association, the three countries agreed to exert their best endeavours to bring the claim to a just and expeditious solution by peaceful means, such as negotiation, conciliation, arbitration, or judicial settlement as well as other peaceful means of the parties' own choice, in conformity with the Charter of the United Nations and the Bandung Declaration.[12]

It must be recalled that for more than a year the British and the Malayans had been negotiating the formation of Malaysia. They had conducted consultations in the Borneo territories, starting 19 February 1962, in what was known as the Cobbold Commission, after its chairman, Lord Cobbold, a former head of the Bank of England. Other members were Wong Pow Nee, Chief Minister of Penang; Ghazali Shafie, Permanent Secretary for External Affairs; Anthony Abell, former Governor of Sarawak; and David Watherston, former Chief Secretary of Malaya. According to its report, issued on 1 August 1962, the Commission interviewed more than 4,000 persons in fifty hearings at twenty centres in Sarawak and fifteen in North Borneo.[13]

The report concluded, although without absolute certainty, that the majority of the people in the Borneo territories favoured their inclusion in the proposed Federation of Malaysia. It said:

143. In assessing the opinion of the peoples of North Borneo and Sarawak we have only been able to arrive at an approximation. We do not wish to make any guarantee that it may not change in one direction or the other in the future. Making allowance for all the difficulties and for our inability to reach every part of these large territories, we have arrived at a general consensus of opinion with reasonable confidence, based on individual and representative evidence presented before us.

144. Although, in such circumstances, individual judgment is bound to vary in emphasis, the Commission as a whole endorse, as a general approximation not far wide of the mark, the following assessment which is made by the Chairman. About one-third of the population in each territory strongly favours early realisation of Malaysia without too much concern about terms and conditions. Another third, many of them favourable to the Malaysia project, ask, with varying degrees of emphasis, for conditions and safeguards varying in nature and extent.... The remaining third is divided between those who insist on independence before Malaysia is considered and those who would strongly prefer to see British rule continue for some years to

come. If the conditions and reservations which they have put forward could be substantially met, the second category referred to above would generally support the proposals. Moreover once a firm decision was taken quite a number of the third category would be likely to abandon their opposition and decide to make the best of a doubtful job....[14]

Ghazali, the chief Malaysian negotiator with the Philippines in the 1960s, was to write later:

Thus, it had taken twenty-one months for the Borneo leaders to make up their minds on Malaysia. The willingness to explore the possibilities of a union with Malaya began with the attendance of Borneo leaders in the Commonwealth Parliamentary Association Conference in July 1961; their continued interest in Malaysia meant four meetings of the Malaysia Solidarity Consultative Committee from August 1961 to January 1962; from February to April 1962 the Cobbold Commission gave official sanction to North Borneo and Sarawak joining Malaysia; and, now twenty-one months later with the adoption (including by the Sarawak and North Borneo legislatures) of the IGC (Inter-governmental Committee, in which the British, Malayan, Sarawak and North Borneo governments were represented and which was chaired by Lord Landsdowne, Britain's Minister of State for the Colonies) Report, the way was clear for Malaysia (parenthetical explanations added).[15]

On 9 July 1963, the Malaysia Agreement was signed in London calling for the formation of the new Federation of Malaysia on 31 August 1963. However, Tunku Abdul Rahman, with the support of the Malayan Cabinet, pushed the date to 16 September, so as to allow the UN mission to go through the "ascertainment" called for at the Manila summit. A mission of nine UN Secretariat officials led by Laurence Michelmore of the United States conducted consultations in Sabah and Sarawak, starting on 26 August. On 14 September 1963, the Secretary-General, U Thant, announced that, on the basis of the mission's report, a majority of the inhabitants of the two territories favoured federation within Malaysia. Two days later, Malaysia was proclaimed.

In his October 1963 UN address, López cited a number of circumstances that had led the Philippines — and Indonesia — to question the conduct and results of the ascertainment process. The timetable of the ascertainment had been reduced from four-to-six weeks to ten working days. Philippine and Indonesian observers were able to witness only the last three days of the process. The Filipinos and the British haggled at length over the number and ranks of the Philippine observers. The British had refused a landing clearance to the aircraft that was to fly those observers to Borneo. To top it all, said López, the U.K. had announced during the ascertainment process that the Federation of Malaysia would be proclaimed on 16 September, as indeed it was and as had been envisioned and publicly declared, regardless of the outcome of the ascertainment. Ghazali has insisted that "the exercise was to enable Jakarta and Manila to welcome Malaysia and not for the purpose of the establishment of Malaysia.[16]

Not surprisingly, the Philippines, together with Indonesia, withheld recognition of the new Federation. Diplomatic relations between Manila and Kuala Lumpur were then suspended. The period from September 1963 to May 1964, when the Philippines re-opened a consulate in Kuala Lumpur, was thus one of tension and mutual recrimination in the relationship between the two countries.

Ghazali was to dismiss the Philippine arguments as "a cartographic claim based on some vague historical ground".[17] In a speech at the National Press Club in Kuala Lumpur on 6 November 1968, Ghazali had called the Philippine claim "absurd" and "not very credible". Addressing and brushing aside the Philippines' legal arguments, invocations of national and regional security, and protestations of peaceful intentions, Ghazali concluded that what the Philippines ultimately wanted was to have Sabah for itself at any cost.[18]

The Indonesian response to the Malaysia proposal was more forceful, but shorter-lived, than that of the Philippines. In January 1963, President Sukarno announced the launch of an Indonesian policy of *konfrontasi* against the proposal on the ground that the project was a "neo-colonialist" plot to enable the British to remain in their former colonies, as the Dutch had tried to do in Indonesia itself, and threaten Indonesia's unity and independence. With Indonesia still insecure about its territorial integrity, Jakarta feared that Malaysia might also absorb Indonesian territory, most prominently Sumatra and Sulawesi. The Indonesian aim evidently was to forestall or at least delay the formation of Malaysia. When Malaysia was nevertheless formed in September 1963, the policy was embodied in the slogan "*Ganjang* (Crush) Malaysia!"

The Indonesian policy of *konfrontasi*, a policy of hostility and opposition including the use of violence but short of open war, had been initiated in the campaign to take West Irian shortly before its application to the very different issue of Malaysia. It had two strands — the diplomatic and the military. The diplomatic strand took the form of increasingly hostile public statements against the Malaysia project and of proposals for schemes designed as substitutes for it, including the still-born confederation of Malay peoples, or MAPHILINDO, which the Philippines had helped initiate. The military was manifested in cross-border raids on Borneo, landings of commandos on the Malay peninsula, sabotage in and incursions into Singapore, as well as Malaya, and the mobilization of "volunteers". Mohd Abu Bakar of the University of Malaya has called the combination of the two strands "coercive bargaining".[19]

According to a declassified "memorandum of conversation" in the archives of the U.S. Department of State, Ghazali had talks in Washington, D.C., on 23 July 1964 with W. Averell Harriman, Undersecretary of State for Political Affairs, William P. Bundy, Assistant Secretary for Far Eastern Affairs, and James Bell, U.S. ambassador to Malaysia. He was reported to have said that Malaysia would have problems agreeing in advance to submit the Sabah dispute with the Philippines to the International Court of Justice, as that would require the concurrence of the Sabah legislature. However, he noted that "Philippine opposition to Malaysia had tapered off, and was not a problem any longer".[20]

Indeed, in May 1964, consular relations had been resumed, with a Philippine consulate being established in Kuala Lumpur, following a bilateral summit meeting between President Macapagal and Malaysian Prime Minister Tunku Abdul Rahman in Phnom Penh in February. A tripartite summit with Indonesian President Sukarno then took place, in June in Tokyo, in which Macapagal assumed the role of mediator between Malaysia and Indonesia, without much success in terms of alleviating Indonesia's hostility to the Malaysia project.

In early June 1966, following the election of Ferdinand Marcos to the Philippine presidency, Malaysia and the Philippines re-opened full embassies in each other's capital after issuing a joint communiqué in which they "agreed to abide by the Manila Accord of 31 July 1963 and with the Joint Statement accompanying it, for the peaceful settlement of the Philippine claim to Sabah". The communiqué said that the two governments "have also recognized the need of sitting together, for the purpose of clarifying the claim and discussing the means of settling it to the satisfaction of both parties."[21] The next year, in September, the two countries concluded an anti-smuggling cooperation agreement that recognised the authority of the Malaysian government to perform official functions in Sabah and under which Philippine customs officials were posted in Kota Kinabalu, Semporna and Sandakan, all cities in Sabah. The protocol to that agreement defined the "Malaysian Border Area" as "the Administrative Districts of Sandakan, Lahad Datu, Semporna, Kudat and Tawau in the State of Sabah".[22]

On 30 September 1965, anticipating the death or incapacity of the ageing Sukarno, the Indonesian Communist Party and the bulk of Indonesia's military apparently raced for the succession, a development that led to a national bloodbath and the eventual takeover — officially in March 1966 — of the presidency by Major General Soeharto. The advent of Soeharto's New Order in Indonesia brought with it a reversal of the national policy from flamboyant nationalism to pragmatic linkage with the international community, from political posturing on the world stage to the pursuit of economic development at home, from confrontation to regional cooperation. The transformation of Indonesia made possible the creation, in August 1967, of a new regional association that would transcend the purposes, as well as surpass the size of the membership, of both the Association of Southeast Asia (ASA) and MAPHILINDO. The new group, the Association of Southeast Asian Nations, or ASEAN, would promote peace among its members, keep Southeast Asia out of the quarrels of the strong, strengthen stability in the region, and eventually gather all of Southeast Asia under its wing.

The reversal of Indonesia's policy and international posture led to the end, formally in August 1966, of the policy of *konfrontasi*. This development was arranged partly in secret talks between Ghazali of Malaysia and Generals Ali Moertopo and Benny Moerdani of Indonesia. ASEAN's formation has given its members, not least Malaysia and the Philippines, an additional motivation for not allowing bilateral disputes to get in the way of regional peace, stability and cooperation.

JABIDAH AND THE BASELINES AMENDMENT

Although not formally dropped, the Philippines' claim to Sabah seemed to be receding as a bone in the throat of Philippines-Malaysia relations. However, in March 1968, less than a year after ASEAN's founding, media reports disclosed the massacre of some twenty-eight to sixty-four or more (the exact number remains undetermined) young, mostly Muslim military recruits on the island of Corregidor at the mouth of Manila Bay on 18 March. Only one, Jibin Arula, then twenty-seven, survived by escaping, although with a bullet wound on his left knee, and swimming — or clinging to driftwood in the sea — for four hours until rescued by passing fishermen. According to Arula, in an interview that he gave to the Philippine media on Corregidor on 18 March 2008, the fortieth anniversary of the massacre,[23] he and his fellow-recruits in the commando unit named Jabidah had been brought to Corregidor on 3 January 1968 for further training. They had been undergoing training in guerrilla warfare in Simunul, an island in the country's extreme south. Other accounts say that they had been enticed by the prospects of monetary compensation and of integration into an elite military unit.

Arula was reported to have recalled that the recruits had written a letter to the office of the President complaining about the bad food (mostly dried fish) and the women whom, they alleged, their officers had brought to Corregidor. Others have claimed that the recruits' grievances also included the non-payment of the promised compensation and the possibility that Oplan Merdeka (freedom), as the secret endeavour was called, would entail killing fellow-Muslims and even the recruits' Tausug and Samal relatives in an attempt to infiltrate Sabah. The revelation of what was supposed to be the real purpose of the training and the interception of the letter of complaint are said to have instigated the massacre at the island's airfield. The most prominent of the Philippine military officers involved was Major Eduardo "Abdul Latif" Martelino, who had converted — or pretended to convert — to Islam. A personality shrouded in mystery and draped with a certain glamour, Martelino dropped out of sight after a couple of fruitless congressional inquiries into the affair.

As a result of the Jabidah fiasco, after months of tense relations featuring demonstrations, flag-burning, boat seizures, arrests, military muscle-flexing, diplomatic protests and counter-protests, inflammatory media stories, and a fruitless and acrimonious meeting in Bangkok in June and July, Malaysia towards the end of September 1968 "suspended" diplomatic relations with the Philippines and withdrew its ambassador from Manila. The Philippines responded in kind.

To make matters worse from the Malaysian point of view, the Philippine Congress, in September, had passed, and President Marcos signed, a bill amending the 1961 baselines law in order to "correct typographical errors" in it. In the process, the Congress tacked on after the corrected coordinates of the baselines a section making explicit reference to the Sabah claim. The added section 2 stated:

> The definition of the baselines of the territorial sea of the Philippine Archipelago as provided in this Act is without prejudice to the delineation of the baselines of the territorial sea around the territory of Sabah, situated in North Borneo, over which the Republic of the Philippines has acquired dominion and sovereignty.[24]

The meaning of the last relative clause was ambiguous. One could interpret it in either of two ways. One is that the Philippines *has* acquired dominion and sovereignty over the cited "territory of Sabah". The other way is to limit the reference to "the territory of Sabah" to that part of Sabah over which the Philippines "has acquired dominion and sovereignty" without signifying whether it has actually been or is still to be acquired.

In any case, Narciso Ramos, Secretary of Foreign Affairs of the Philippines, explained to the UN General Assembly on 15 October 1968:

The old law did not include Sabah within Philippine territory. Neither does the new law. In other words, if a new Philippine map were plotted today based on the technical description contained in the new law, Sabah would lie outside that map....

The "delineation" spoken of in section 2 of the new law is a future delineation which would be made should the Philippines recover Sabah. In other words, if Malaysia agrees to have the dispute elevated to the (International) Court (of Justice) and if that tribunal decides in favour of the Philippines, then a delineation of the new baselines will be made....

The law in question was passed in response to a United Nations request for the updating of publications on the law of the sea in the Organization's "Legislative Series" under publication. Section 2 was inserted in order to protect the Philippine claim and avoid the possible charge that the Philippines has by law implicitly waived the claim by failing to include Sabah's waters in the delimitation of the Philippine territorial sea... .

The statement in Section 2 of the new law that the "Republic of the Philippines has acquired dominion and sovereignty" over Sabah is not new. It is a restatement of the official position of the Philippines announced many times before....[25]

Similarly, ten days later, Senator Arturo Tolentino, a member of the Philippine delegation to the General Assembly, in reply to Malaysian statements, explained that the reference in section 2 of the new law to "the delineation of the baselines of the territorial sea around the territory of Sabah" meant "the future delineation" and did not in itself make Sabah a part of the Philippines.[26] Nevertheless, it did make clear the possibility of the claim being pursued.

It may be recalled that, in the debate in the House of Representatives on the 1961 baselines law, many of those who voted against its passage and explained their votes cited its possible impact on the Philippine claim to North Borneo as the reason for their dissent.[27] This, notwithstanding the later argument, notably by Tolentino, that the 1961 baselines law could not have contained any reference to North Borneo, as the cession by the Sultan of Sulu, Esmail Kiram, of his North Borneo territories to the Philippine government had not taken place until April 1962.

In December 1968, the ASEAN foreign ministers took the unusual step of all five of them attending a meeting of the UN Economic Commission for Asia and the Far East (ECAFE), later renamed the UN Economic and Social Commission for Asia and the Pacific (ESCAP), in Bangkok. The Thai foreign minister then invited his Malaysian and Philippine counterparts to Bangsaen, on the Gulf of Thailand, where the two agreed on yet another "cooling-off period".[28]

Reporting on the address of Malaysia's Prime Minister opening the third ASEAN Ministerial Meeting in the Cameron Highlands on 16 December 1969, the meeting's joint communiqué said that Tunku Abdul Rahman had "announced that as a result of a discussion between him and the Honorable Mr. Carlos P. Romulo, Secretary of Foreign Affairs of the Philippines, in the spirit of goodwill and friendship and because of the great value Malaysia and the Philippines placed on ASEAN, it was agreed that diplomatic relations between Malaysia and the Philippines would be normalised forthwith and that the ambassadors of their respective countries would be appointed".[29]

Diplomatic relations between the two countries were formally resumed, and the overall relationship has been "normalised". Because of developments in Southeast Asia and in the larger region, as well as in Malaysia and the Philippines, the issue of regional security — whether it would be served better if Sabah were in Malaysia or in the Philippines — has long receded into irrelevance. Philippine leaders, however, have found it politically impossible formally to drop the Philippine claim to Sabah altogether.

DROPPING THE PHILIPPINE CLAIM?

At the second ASEAN Summit, in Kuala Lumpur in August 1977, President Marcos declared to loud applause, "As a contribution, therefore, I say in earnest to the future of ASEAN, I wish to announce that the Government of the Republic of the Philippines is therefore taking definite steps to eliminate one of the burdens of ASEAN — the claim of the Philippine Republic to Sabah."

During the debates in the 1986 Constitutional Commission, Blas Ople, one of the commissioners, is recorded as having declared that President Marcos had taken this action upon the recommendation of three foreign ministers — Emmanuel Peláez, Carlos P. Romulo and Arturo Tolentino — "because the claim had become self-defeating in terms of national objectives". The report of the Committee on Preamble, National Territory and Declaration of Principles continues, "Besides, Mr. Ople pointed out that when the United Nations conducted a referendum in 1963 at the behest of the Philippine and Indonesian governments, the people of Sabah overwhelmingly voted to become part of Malaysia. He added that the unfriendly atmosphere under which 140,000 Filipinos in Sabah live might exacerbate (sic) because of the claim."[30]

In any case, Marcos made the announcement on taking "definite steps" to drop the Philippine claim to Sabah at an ASEAN summit in order to gain maximum effect and publicity out of it and to do it in a regional context. There is no evidence of any direct impact of Malaysia's and the Philippines' common membership in ASEAN on the Marcos decision, but it could have been one of the considerations for his conciliatory move.

As it turned out, neither Marcos nor any of his successors managed to take those "definite steps" to abandon the claim to Sabah, at least not in terms acceptable to Malaysia. The political pressures to do so were just not enough; the pressures not to do so were too great.

The 1987 Philippine Constitution, the one currently in force, has this provision on the national territory (Article I):

> The national territory comprises the Philippine archipelago, with all the islands and waters embraced therein, and all other territories over which the Philippines has sovereignty or jurisdiction, consisting of its terrestrial, fluvial and aerial domains, including its territorial sea, the seabed, the subsoil, the insular shelves, and other submarine areas. The waters around, between, and connecting the islands of the archipelago, regardless of their breadth and dimensions, form part of the internal waters of the Philippines.[31]

The Constitutional Commission that produced the document had a heated debate, from 26 June to 10 July 1986, on two issues pertaining to this article.[32] One was, again, on whether to have a provision on the national territory at all. The Commission's Committee on Preamble, National Territory and Declaration of Principles had proposed, in part, this definition of the national territory: "The national territory comprises the Philippine archipelago with all the islands and waters embraced therein, and all other territories belonging to the Philippines by historic right or legal title..." This was all but identical to the 1973 Constitution's definition, whose adoption had caused considerable consternation in Malaysia. The other issue arose from an amendment to this proposed provision. Formally put forward in plenary by Father Joaquin Bernas, S.J., the amendment would replace "territories over which the government exercises sovereign jurisdiction", the formulation found in the latest amendment to the original draft in replacement of "by historic right or legal title", with "territories over which the Philippines has sovereignty or jurisdiction". The significant differences were between "government" and "the Philippines" and between "exercises" and "has".

Both arguments revolved around whether either proposal would mean keeping the door open to the Philippines claiming Sabah in the future or foreclosing such a move and whether it would advance or weaken the claim. Some commissioners, like Father Bernas, were evidently concerned that any formulation that could be read as restaking a claim to Sabah would not only be unhelpful to the claim but would disrupt relations with Malaysia and with the rest of ASEAN once more. They insisted that, while the proposed formulation would not close the door to the future pursuit of such a claim, it would, in Father Bernas's word, "prescind" from the issue. It would be better, it was pointed out, to leave it to the Executive to decide on the matter. The provision on the national territory, with the Bernas amendment, was approved.

Nevertheless, the Malaysians remained suspicious both of the constitutional provision on the national territory, even with the Bernas formulation, and, more so, of section 2 of the 1968 amendment to the baselines act.

In quiet negotiations that began in the last years of the Marcos administration, after Mahathir Mohamad had taken over Malaysia's political leadership, and continued in the first years of the succeeding Aquino administration, the Philippines proposed to settle the issue of sovereignty over Sabah by an amendment to section 2 of the 1968 baselines law or by some other legislative act. In return, Malaysia would sign agreements on amity, cooperation and commercial relations, extradition, border crossing, and joint patrol with the Philippines by the time of the ASEAN Summit in Manila in December 1987.

Early in 1987, Michael Mastura, an intellectual Muslim Maguindanao congressman, filed a bill in the House of Representatives that would amend section 2 of the 1968 baselines law to read:

> Section 2. The definition of the baselines of the territorial sea of the Philippine Archipelago as provided in this Act is without prejudice to the Philippine negotiating text on boundary delimitations under the United Nations Law of the Sea Convention.

The removal of the reference to the Sabah claim was meant to fulfill the Philippine commitments in the negotiations with Malaysia. The Malaysians were so informed.

The Speaker of the House, the late Ramon Mitra, a close ally of the President, took the unusual step of descending from the rostrum and speaking in support of the bill and of the benefits that would accrue to the Philippines from refraining from the pursuit of its claim to Sabah under the terms being negotiated. He asked:

(H)as anybody ever quantified how much it has cost us to pursue this claim? Has anybody ever cited any figure on the losses which we have sustained because one part of the country cannot pursue any legitimate trade with Sabah …?

And has anybody ever thought or told our countrymen about the great influence of a hostile Sabah over the insurgency problem in the South, in Sabah where they train those who come to the Philippines and inflame the spirits of those who fight against the Republic? We do not know. And has anybody cared about the 100,000 Filipinos who are … in Sabah and who are bereft of any kind of government support because we hold the fiction that Sabah is part of the Philippines and, therefore, cannot set up any kind of government entity (there)?

Mitra continued:

(I)t is obvious that we cannot occupy Sabah. Nor would we want to occupy Sabah. I am sure it would never get anywhere if such an idea were presented….

Yes, … this is intended to foster a closer and lasting relationship with our closest neighbor. Yes, this is an act by this Body to assume responsibility for the solution of this problem. Yes, we are standing up to accept the challenge that this generation of Filipinos is prepared to assume the consequences and to tell the coming generations that, in this age, we stood up and decided what may not be popular but what we believe is the correct step that we should take in order to end this problem that cries out for a solution.[33]

On 3 December, the Malaysian foreign minister, Abu Hassan Omar, announced that the Malaysian Cabinet had decided to conclude agreements with the Philippines on friendship and cooperation and on joint border patrol and border crossing "following the successful passage of legislation in the Philippines that would definitively drop its claim (to Sabah) and invalidate any decree related to the claim".[34]

The House of Representatives approved the Mastura bill on 10 December 1987. The Philippine government's moves, however, were floundering in the Senate. There, the Mastura bill was set aside. A bill filed by Senator Leticia Ramos-Shahani with the support of President Aquino, which would adjust the Philippines' archipelagic baselines but would not carry any provision referring to Sabah, encountered furious opposition. Later, Senate President Jovito Salonga and fourteen other senators, a clear majority of the twenty-four-member Senate, filed a legislative proposal similar to the Mastura bill but with the addition of three sets of conditions, including some of the understandings arrived at in the negotiations with Malaysia. These conditions were the ratification of the treaties on amity, cooperation and commercial relations, which had already been initialed, and on extradition; the conclusion of the border-crossing and border-patrol agreements, also initialed, and of the economic agreements specified in the treaty of amity, cooperation and commercial relations; and "the full and satisfactory settlement of the proprietary claims of the heirs of the Sultanate (sic) of Sulu".[35] Malaysia had all along opposed any explicit and conditional linkage between legislative action on the Sabah claim and the conclusion of the agreements of interest to the Philippines.

At the same time, senior Malaysian leaders had been expressing their government's willingness to pay a certain sum to the heirs of Sultan Jamalul Kiram II in settlement of their proprietary claim. For example, the Malaysian foreign minister said on 26 November 1987:

> It is also noted that the current congressional deliberations in the Philippines has (sic) given rise to expressions of concern on the proprietary rights of the heirs of the Sultan of Sulu. This is a matter to be considered between the Malaysian Government and the rightful Sulu heirs. Malaysia has always lived up to its commitments emanating from the Macaskie Judgement of 1939 and is prepared to consider all avenues for a satisfactory resolution of this question.[36]

However, Malaysia needed to know from the Philippine government with whom Kuala Lumpur was to deal with respect to the sum involved and the heirs concerned. Accordingly, Aquino convened in Malacañang Palace on 4 December 1987 a meeting among the descendants of the nine individuals whom Judge Macaskie had designated as heirs of Sultan Jamalul Kiram II. Also in attendance were Abraham Rasul and his wife, Senator Santanina Rasul. Abraham Rasul claimed to be a descendant of Jamalul Kiram II and the *wazir* (equivalent to Prime Minister) of the Sulu Sultanate's Ruma Bechara. After much discussion, the assemblage, around forty persons in all, settled on Raul S. Manglapus, then the Philippines' Secretary of Foreign Affairs, as the heirs' interlocutor with Malaysia. Manglapus accepted the designation provided he did not receive any compensation for his efforts. The whole project was soon scuttled by bickering among those claiming to be heirs.

NORMALIZING PHILIPPINES-MALAYSIA RELATIONS

After the change of leadership in the Philippines in 1992, I, as Undersecretary of Foreign Affairs, accompanied the then Secretary of Foreign Affairs, Roberto R. Romulo, on an official visit to Malaysia in September. We naturally called on Abdullah Ahmad Badawi, then Malaysia's Foreign Minister, at his old Wisma Putra office in Kuala Lumpur. As we were leaving, the minister asked, with apparent casualness, "So, when is your President coming to visit?" I could hardly believe my ears. If President Fidel V. Ramos were to go to Malaysia, it would be the first state or official visit by a Philippine President since President Marcos' journey to that country in January 1968 (not counting Marcos' attendance at the funeral of Malaysia's late Prime Minister, Abdul Razak, in 1976). Since the March 1978 visit to Manila of Malaysia's federal monarch, the Yang di-Pertuan Agong, who, in any case, was not a political leader,[37] the Philippines and Malaysia had refrained from exchanging high-level visits on account of the Sabah dispute. When we returned to the Philippine Embassy at No. 1 Changkat Kia Peng, I telephoned Halim Ali, then the Deputy Secretary-General of the Ministry of Foreign Affairs, who had been present at our meeting with the minister. Halim, who was later to be appointed Chief Secretary to the Malaysian government, confirmed that, indeed, President Ramos would be welcome to make a visit to Malaysia and that he, Halim, would be happy to discuss its "timing".

Thus, in what was clearly a historic event, President Ramos was, in January 1993, welcomed to Kuala Lumpur as a state visitor, with all the pomp and pageantry that such occasions normally call for. The next year, in February 1994, Prime Minister Mahathir Mohamad returned the visit. Ramos proposed that the sum offered by Malaysia go not just to one extended family but to the development of the Sulu area as a whole. In April, the Yang di-Pertuan Agong paid a state visit to the Philippines. For all practical purposes, Philippine-Malaysian relations had returned to normal, with Sabah having settled in as a state of Malaysia.

It is not certain what exactly prompted Malaysia's willingness to host Ramos as the ultimate symbol of reconciliation over the technically unsettled dispute over Sabah, but it is possible to speculate that Kuala Lumpur, at the beginning of a new leadership in the Philippines, saw an opportunity to mend fences with a next-door neighbour and firm up the Philippines' tendency to leave dormant, *de facto* if not *de jure*, its claim to parts of Sabah.

One factor favouring Malaysia was that internationally it had the backing of militarily potent countries, such as Canada, Australia and New Zealand, as well as Great Britain, while the Philippines had none in the pursuit of its claim. Politically, the international community has generally accepted Malaysian ownership of Sabah. The Philippine claim has received no such support. Since the overthrow of President Sukarno, even Indonesia has withdrawn its opposition to Malaysia.

PRESSING THE PHILIPPINE CLAIM

However, the Philippine claim has occasionally surfaced to roil Philippine-Malaysian relations even after the Marcos regime. In one of the most recent of those occasions, the Philippines, in March 2001, applied for permission to intervene in the case on sovereignty over the small islands of Sipadan and Ligitan off Sabah, which Malaysia held and Indonesia, as well as Malaysia, claimed. Indonesia and Malaysia had agreed, in May 1997, to submit the dispute to the International Court of Justice (ICJ) in The Hague for adjudication. The Philippines' application to intervene was based on its desire, as it told the Court, "to preserve and safeguard the historical and legal rights of ... the Philippines arising from its claim to dominion and sovereignty over the territory of North Borneo, to the extent that these rights are affected, or may be affected, by a determination of the Court". The Philippines made it clear that it "does not seek to become a party to the dispute before the Court concerning sovereignty over Pulau Ligitan and Pulau Sipadan".[38]

Both Indonesia and Malaysia opposed the Philippine application. As Agent and leader of Indonesia's delegation, Hassan Wirajuda, then Director-General for Political Affairs at the Department of Foreign Affairs and later Minister of Foreign Affairs, cited the lateness of the filing of the Philippines' application, the approval of which, he argued, would lead to further delay in the proceedings on the main Sipadan-Ligitan case. The Malaysians, led by Tan Sri Abdul Kadir Mohamad, Secretary-General of the Ministry of Foreign Affairs, acting as Agent, and their counsel and advocates denied the Philippines' contention that it had an "interest of a legal nature" in the case before the Court. In the process, they summarised the Malaysian position on the Philippine claim to parts of Sabah in rebuttal of the Philippines' arguments. They also argued that the Philippine application for permission to intervene was a "distraction".

In the end, on 23 October 2001, the Court, by a vote of fourteen to one, decided to deny the Philippine application. In its ruling, the Court declared that the Philippines had failed to convince it that "specified legal interests may be affected in the particular circumstances of this case." Nevertheless, the Court continued, it "remains cognizant of the positions stated before it by Indonesia, Malaysia and the Philippines in the present proceedings."[39] Judge Shigeru Oda appended his lone dissenting opinion to the Court's decision.[40] Although it lost its case, the Philippines had managed to raise arguments in support of its Sabah claim at the ICJ, whose ruling on the claim it had long sought to obtain. On the other hand, Malaysia had had the opportunity to respond to those arguments before the same Court.

In the main case, the Court eventually, on 17 December 2002, ruled, 16–1, in favour of Malaysia, which had been in control of the two islands. The lone dissenting vote was that of Judge *ad hoc* Thomas Franck, whom Indonesia had appointed in pursuance of Article 31 of the Court's Statutes.[41] Through its ruling, the ICJ showed once again its tendency in territorial issues not to change radically the actual realities on the ground.

CONCLUSIONS

As for the Philippine claim to a portion of North Borneo, the legal issues between the Philippines and Malaysia seem to be joined. The Philippines insists that the document by which the Sultan of Sulu, Jamalul Alam, turned over that portion of North Borneo to Overbeck and Dent was one of lease, albeit "forever and until the end of time", subject to an annual rental, while Malaysia regards it as one of cession or sale. Malaysia considers the Sultanate of Sulu to have disappeared as a sovereign entity in 1878, when Spain finally succeeded in conquering it, or in 1915, with the conclusion of the Carpenter Agreement, or in 1936, with the death of Sultan Jamalul Kiram II. The Philippines, on the other hand, regards the Sultanate as having subsisted at least until April 1962, when Sultan Mohammad Esmail Kiram "ceded and transferred" Sulu's purported territory in North Borneo to the Philippine Republic. Malaysia recognizes the sovereign rights that Great Britain exercised in Sabah before that territory's inclusion in the new Federation of Malaysia in 1963. The Philippines disputes such sovereign rights and, therefore, Britain's inability to bequeath sovereignty to Malaysia. Malaysia has stressed that the consultations conducted in Sabah, as well as Sarawak, reflected the desire of the people of the Borneo territories to be part of Malaysia. The Philippines has insisted that those consultations did not constitute the "fresh approach" called for by the 1963 Manila Accord. Malaysia affirms the validity of the ascertainment that the United Nations conducted in Sabah — and Sarawak — just before the formation of Malaysia. The Philippines has questioned it, as did Sukarno's Indonesia.

Irrespective of the legal arguments on both sides, however, the facts unfolding on the ground have indicated a steady strengthening of Kuala Lumpur's hold on the territory. Elections under Malaysian auspices have been held regularly in Sabah for federal, as well as state, offices. Malaysian politics are constantly played out in the state. Malaysian federal immigration, customs and police officers operate in Sabah, including in the arrest of Filipino suspects and periodic crackdowns on undocumented Filipinos. The Philippine government deals with those officers in discharging its consular functions on behalf of Filipinos in a foreign land. For the first time, Malaysia has a Sabah-born foreign minister in Anifah Hj. Aman, who assumed that office in April 2009. Malaysian authorities have cited the exchange of ambassadors and the anti-smuggling and other agreements between the two countries as manifestations of the Philippines' recognition of Malaysian sovereignty over Sabah. Not least, all other countries of the world acknowledge it.

Conceivably more fundamental than the conflicting legal positions is the asymmetry arising from the realities on the ground as against the Philippines' legal arguments. Assuming without necessarily conceding, to use a phrase favoured by lawyers and logicians, the validity of the Philippines' legal claims, which Malaysia, of course, rejects, the legal title collides with the political and demographic realities, including the reality of "effective occupation", legal technicalities with actual control, legal right with the fact that no other state supports that right or questions Malaysia's position, the law with *realpolitik*.

On the other hand, it is extremely difficult for any Philippine politician to even appear to be dropping the Philippine claim or making concessions on it. Presidents Aquino and Ramos tried it, as they sought to stabilize and improve relations with Malaysia and secure for the heirs of the Sultan of Sulu and for the Sulu area the material compensation that the Malaysian government was offering. However, they were stymied by fellow-politicians. Filipinos who pay heed to the issue have been clearly divided on the Sabah claim. Nationalist fervor keeps getting in the way of any move by the President to seek a resolution to or even compromises on it. Trying to score domestic political points or acting out of more noble motives, politicians would surely seize any such move as an opportunity to transform for public presentation an extremely complex issue into a simple matter. Others seek to get this vexing problem with a neighbour out of the way and move on.

Francisco Tatad sagely said on the floor of the Philippine Senate in October 1992:

> For all intents and purposes, the claim is dead; it was probably stillborn. There is no need for any of the parties to do anything about it, either to revive it, which may be an impossibility, or to arrange for its formal burial, which may be a superfluity. Let sleeping dogs lie. No better policy offers itself at this time. The claim is not, and need not be, an obstacle to genuine cooperation between Malaysia and the Philippines. They should proceed, like other countries afflicted with similar disputes, as though the claim did not exist at all.[42]

In the meantime, however, the Philippines is unable to establish a consulate in Sabah, an event that would further indicate a recognition by the Philippines of the legitimacy of North Borneo's place under Malaysia's sovereignty. Many sectors have clamoured for a Philippine consulate in Sabah. The Philippine foreign service, led by the embassy in Kuala Lumpur, has for years sought to establish one so as to enhance its ability to protect the hundreds of thousands of Filipinos living in Sabah — legally or illegally — and extend other consular services to them. In June 2000, Secretary of Foreign Affairs Domingo Siazon was quoted as saying, "The best way to deal with the more than 500,000 Filipinos in Sabah is to have an office at Kota Kinabalu."[43] The numerous Filipinos living in the territory have called for a consulate in the Sabah capital for the same reason. The state government of Sabah has been pressing the Philippine government to set up one in order to help manage the problems arising from the presence of so many Filipinos in the state. So have non-governmental organizations dealing with human rights or human trafficking or both. *Malaysiakini* quoted Suhakam, the human-rights commission of Malaysia, in October 2008 as urging the Philippines to establish a consulate in Sabah to speed up the issuance of travel documents to Filipinos detained in the state for illegal entry or overstaying.[44] In 1995, the Philippine and Malaysian governments agreed to open consulates in Sabah and Davao. The Malaysians opened their outpost in Davao in southern Mindanao in December 1995; the Philippines has not carried out its part of the deal.

The Philippines has tried a number of ways to establish some kind of practical presence in East Malaysia short of an official consulate, to no avail. One was a proposal to open a consulate in Labuan, a group of islands off Sabah, which the state had ceded to the federal government in 1984 and which was thus no longer part of Sabah. Another was for the Philippine embassy in Kuala Lumpur to establish an informal but operational office in Kota Kinabalu. In the early 1990s, the Philippine embassy rented office premises in Kota Kinabalu from which to serve the growing Filipino community. However, Malaysia's federal authorities asked the Philippines to desist. A compromise seems to have been reached in the form of deployments of up to 30 days of four to eight Filipino personnel to extend passport and other consular services to Filipinos in Sabah out of hotels in Kota Kinabalu, Sandakan, and, occasionally, Tawau and Lahad Datu.

The negotiations on the delimitation of the maritime boundary between the Philippines and Indonesia, that is, at the area where their respective territorial waters and exclusive economic zones overlap, have had to stop at the point where Malaysian waters as projected from Sabah intersect with those of the Philippines and Indonesia. The result is that Indonesia has been unable to complete the delineation of the maritime boundaries around its archipelago and thus definitively define its contours. So has the Philippines.

Not least, the descendants of Sultan Jamalul Kiram II and their community in Sulu have been unable to enjoy the fruits of any compensation offered by Malaysia for their proprietary claims.

Notes

1. The documents quoted in this and subsequent paragraphs on the Philippine claim to Sabah are compiled in *The Philippine Claim to a Portion of North Borneo: Materials and Documents* (Diliman, Quezon City: Institute of International Legal Studies, University of the Philippines Law Center, 2003).
2. "Committee Report No. 3 on Proposed Resolution No. 263 on National Territory: Deliberations of 26 June 1986", in Raphael Perpetuo M. Lotilla, ed., *The Philippine National Territory: A Collection of Related Documents* (Diliman, Quezon City: Institute of International Legal Studies, University of the Philippines Law Center, and Manila: Foreign Service Institute, Department of Foreign Affairs, 1995), p. 556.
3. *The Philippine Claim to a Portion of North Borneo*, p. 78.
4. Ibid., pp. 142–44.
5. Ibid., p. 106.
6. Nicholas Tarling, *Southeast Asia and the Great Powers* (Oxon and New York: Routledge, 2010), p. 77.
7. J. A. C. Mackie, *Konfrontasi: The Indonesia-Malaysia Dispute 1963–1966* (Kuala Lumpur: Oxford University Press, 1974), pp. 6–7.
8. *The Philippine Claim to a Portion of North Borneo*, pp. 108–109.
9. Ibid., pp. 117–25.
10. Tarling, *Southeast Asia and the Great Powers*, p. 59.
11. *The Philippine Claim to a Portion of North Borneo*, pp. 148–67.
12. <http://untreaty.un.org/unts/1_60000/16/16/00030780.pdf>.
13. <http://www.digitalibrary.my/dmdocuments/malaysiakini/767_Report%20of% 20the%20Commission% 20 of%20EnquiryNorth%20Borneo%20&%20Saraw ak%20&%20IGC%201962.pdf>, p. 8.
14. Ibid., pp. 44 and 45.
15. Ghazali Shafie, *Memoir on the Formation of Malaysia* (Bangi, Selangor, Malaysia: Universiti Kebangsaan Malaysia, 1998), p. 326.
16. Ibid., p. 432.
17. Ibid., p. 27.
18. Ghazali Shafie, "The Manila Claim in Perspective", in M. Ghazali bin Shafie, *Malaysia: International Relations* (Kuala Lumpur: Creative Enterprise Sendirian Berhad, 1982), pp. 142–52.

19. Mohd. Abu Bakar: *The Escalation of Konfrontasi (June-September 1964)* (Kuala Lumpur: Universiti Malaya, 1978), pp. 6 and 8.

20. <http://www.gwu.edu/~nsarchiv/NSAEBB/NSAEBB52/doc577.pdf>.

21. Ibid.

22. *The Philippine Claim to a Portion of North Borneo*, pp. 182–89.

23. <http://newsinfo.inquirer.net/breakingnews/nation/view/20080318-125522/Lone-survivor-recalls-Jabidah-Massacre>.

24. Lotilla, ed., *The Philippine National Territory*, p. 370.

25. *The Philippine Claim to a Portion of North Borneo*, pp. 163–64.

26. Arturo M. Tolentino, *Philippine Reply to the Malaysian Statements of 15 and 16 October 1968*, United Nations General Assembly, New York, 25 October 1968 (document in the author's possession).

27. Lotilla, ed., *The Philippine National Territory*, pp. 335–41.

28. Donald Tracy Laird, "The Philippines in Southeast Asia: Transactions, Interactions and Conflict with Indonesia, Malaysia, Singapore and Thailand" (doctoral dissertation, University of Michigan, 1975), p. 252.

29. <http://www.aseansec.org/3690.htm>, No. 2.

30. "Committee Report No. 3 on Proposed Resolution No. 263 on National Territory: Deliberations of 26 June 1986", in Lotilla, ed., *The Philippine National Territory*, p. 556.

31. <http://www.chanrobles.com/article1.htm>.

32. Lotilla, ed., *The Philippine National Territory*, pp. 555–93.

33. Quoted in a document in the author's possession.

34. Quoted in ibid.

35. Ibid.

36. Quoted in ibid.

37. <http://www.philembassykl.org.my/overview.htm>.

38. Ibid., p. 215.

39. The full ruling is in *The Philippine Claim to a Portion of North Borneo*, pp. 369–401.

40. Ibid., pp. 402–12.

41. <http://www.icj-cij.org/docket/files/102/7714.pdf>.

42. Document in the author's possession.

43. <http://www.highbeam.com/doc/1G1-62775071.html>.

44. <http://www.suhakam.org.my/c/document_library/get_file?p_l_id=23805&folderId=26253&name= DLFE-610.pdf>.

5

THE SOUTH CHINA SEA

The Treaty of Peace with Japan, signed in San Francisco on 8 September 1951, states in its Article 2, "Japan renounces all right, title and claim to the Spratly Islands and to the Paracel Islands," which Japanese forces occupied just before and during World War II and from which they launched attacks on other countries in the region. However, the treaty does not say which nation is to have such right, title or claim to those islands, although the Vietnamese have asserted that, since those islands belong to Vietnam, it can be assumed that they reverted to Vietnam after Japan was divested of them.[1] The Chinese have made a similar claim on behalf of Chinese ownership.

The Philippines and Vietnam were among the forty-nine states that signed the treaty. Neither the People's Republic of China, which had taken control of the Chinese mainland almost two years earlier, nor the "Republic of China", which had fled to Taiwan but claimed to be the government of all of China, was invited to the San Francisco conference that produced the treaty. This was mainly because some of the participants in the conference recognized the People's Republic as the rightful government of China, while others continued to give recognition to the authorities on Taiwan as the government of all of China.

On 28 April 1952, the same day that the San Francisco Treaty entered into force, Japan and the "Republic of China", which Japan then considered as the Chinese government, signed a separate Treaty of Peace in Taipei. In it, the two parties "recognized" that, under the San Francisco Treaty, Japan had "renounced all right, title, and claim to Taiwan (Formosa) and Penghu (the Pescadores) as well as the Spratley Islands and the Paracel Islands", again without specifying which nation would have such right, title or claim. On

29 September 1972, Japan shifted its diplomatic relations from Taipei to Beijing by means of the Joint Communiqué issued during Prime Minister Kakuei Tanaka's visit to China. Without explicitly referring to the Paracels or the Spratlys, the communiqué stated that Japan "firmly maintains its stand under Article 8 of the Potsdam Proclamation" issued by the leaders of the Republic of China, the United Kingdom and the United States on 26 July 1945, which limited Japanese sovereignty "to the islands of Honshu, Hokkaido, Kyushu, Shikoku and such minor islands as we determine". Six years later, on 12 August 1978, Japan and the People's Republic signed a Treaty of Peace and Friendship, which reaffirmed the 1972 Joint Communiqué but was otherwise silent on territorial issues.

THE CLOMA CLAIM

Meanwhile, in 1947, fishing boats belonging to Tomás Cloma, a Filipino marine educator and entrepreneur, mainly in fishing-related ventures, started visiting the islands of the South China Sea that are closest to the Philippines. According to A.V.H. Hartendorp, Cloma "considered plans to establish an ice plant and cannery on Itu Aba and also to exploit the guano deposits on the islands."[2]

In 1956, after sending the training ship of his Philippine Maritime Institute on an expedition to the islands in early March, Cloma on 15 May proceeded, through a "Notice to the Whole World", to claim ownership of an area in the South China Sea of 64,976 square nautical miles. The coordinates indicated were roughly congruent with the area that the Philippine government was to claim as Kalayaan twenty-two years later.[3] On the same day, in a letter enclosing the "Notice" and its accompanying maps, Cloma wrote the Secretary of Foreign Affairs, then Vice President Carlos P. García, informing the Philippine government that "about forty citizens of the Philippines were undertaking survey and occupation work 'in a territory in the China Sea outside of Philippine waters and not within the jurisdiction of any country', and that the territory being occupied was being claimed by him and his associates".[4]

Six days later, on 21 May, Cloma sent another letter to the Secretary of Foreign Affairs informing him that the territory that he was claiming had been named "Freedomland" and enclosing a list of the new names that he had given the individual islands and other features. Stressing that the claim to the territory had been made by citizens of the Philippines and not by the Philippine government or on its behalf, Cloma urged the government to support that claim rather than make one of its own lest a government claim invite "opposition from other countries".[5]

From July to September 1956, Cloma issued a flurry of documents, including a "Charter of the Free Territory of Freedomland" on 6 July providing for the country's territory, seal and flag. The territory included "all the islands, islets, isles, atolls, banks, reefs, shoals, fishing grounds and waters" within the set of coordinates laid down in the "Notice" and reiterated in the Charter, without specifying the nature or extent of the fishing grounds and waters. The Charter prescribed the structure of government and adopted all Philippine laws and judicial decisions. It incorporated the Universal Declaration of Human Rights and the Philippine Bill of Rights. An announcement signed by Cloma, a younger brother of his and three of his four sons on 7 July named him "Chairman, Supreme Council of State of Freedomland and Head of State" and two others as "Supreme Solon" and "Supreme Magistrate". A letter sent out by Cloma as "Head of State" on the same day announced the formation of the equivalent of a cabinet. In September, Cloma issued rules on citizenship and on coinage and currency.[6]

In a 6 July press statement, Cloma cited the strategic reasons behind his claim to "Freedomland" and his establishment of an independent state there. He warned that "Red China" could be recognized by the United Nations by the end of the year and thus could take over the claim of Nationalist China. He pointed to the resurgence of Japan, France and England and the rise of "the Vietnams" as other potential sources of threat to the Philippines. An independent "Freedomland", he said, would help avert these threats while sparing the Philippines the legal complications of annexing new territory.[7]

Although Cloma's activities had the whiff of farce — President Ramon Magsaysay has been quoted as calling them "comic opera" in asking Vice President and Secretary of Foreign Affairs García to cut them short[8] — they were taken seriously enough to provoke protests, starting as early as May 1956, from Nationalist China on Taiwan, the Chinese Foreign Ministry in Beijing, Guangming Daily (a Hong Kong Chinese-language newspaper leaning towards the People's Republic of China), France, and South Vietnam (which called Cloma's endeavours a "burlesque adventure"[9]), all asserting opposing claims to all or parts of the area in question. Beyond protests, Nationalist Chinese forces took naval action against the activities of Cloma and his group.

After months of declining to do so, the Philippine government finally adopted a position on the "Freedomland" issue. This took the form of a letter, dated 8 February 1957, by Secretary of Foreign Affairs García in reply to a letter that Cloma had sent President Magsaysay, dated 14 December 1956.

The Cloma letter had complained about Taiwanese activities, reported in the Taipei press, "trying to grab phosphate mining operation which is presently undertaken by us".[10] García carefully limited his response to the views of the Department of Foreign Affairs rather than the Philippine government itself. The Department of Foreign Affairs, he said, "regards the islands, islets, coral reefs, shoals, and sand cays, comprised within what you called 'Freedomland', with the exclusion of those belonging to the seven-island group known internationally as the Spratlys, as *res nullius*", that is, something that does not belong to anyone. This meant, he continued, "that they are open to economic exploitation and settlement by Filipino nationals, ... so long as the exclusive sovereignty of any country over them has not been established". García added that "the Philippine Government considers (the Spratly) islands as under the de facto trusteeship of the Allied Powers of the Second World War, ... there being no territorial settlement made by the Allied Powers ... with respect to their disposition". Finally, the Vice President invoked the Philippines' interest in the islands encompassed by "Freedomland" — their proximity to the Philippines, their historical and geological relations with the archipelago, their strategic value, and their economic potential. However, he took care to refrain from asserting a claim to sovereignty or ownership on the part of the Philippines itself.[11]

THE PHILIPPINE CLAIM

By 1971, the Philippine position seemed to have changed. A communiqué read by President Ferdinand Marcos at a press conference on 10 July 1971 announced the results of discussions at an emergency meeting of the National Security Council on the security implications for the Philippines of the occupation by Taiwanese forces of Itu Aba, referred to as Tai Ping in Chinese and as Ligaw by the Philippines. Repeating the view that "Freedomland" was not part of the Spratlys,[12] the announcement reaffirmed the Philippine position that the Spratlys were "under the *de facto* trusteeship of the allied powers", by virtue of which "no one may introduce troops on any of these islands without the permission and consent of the allied powers". It revealed that the Philippine government had asked Taipei to remove its troops from Itu Aba, since their deployment there did not have the consent of the allies. The Marcos statement reiterated that, on the other hand, "Freedomland" was *res nullius* that could be acquired by "occupation and effective administration". It concluded by announcing that "we are in effective occupation and control of Pagasa (Thitu), Lawak (Nanshan Island) and Patag (Flat Island)".[13] Both Taipei and Beijing immediately issued protests.

On 17 November 1971, Secretary of Foreign Affairs Carlos P. Romulo submitted a memorandum to Marcos recommending, in the light of increasingly dangerous encounters between Philippine and Nationalist Chinese forces in "Freedomland", that the Philippine military presence in the area be augmented. The memorandum urged that the islands be developed and populated, the place used as a penal colony, the Philippine flag kept hoisted in the territory, and Philippine governmental processes extended there. Romulo asserted that these measures would reinforce the Philippine position that "these islands are part of Philippine territory".[14] The Philippines' Undersecretary of Foreign Affairs, José D. Ingles, was to recall that in March 1972 he had asserted at the UN Seabed Committee "the effective occupation by the Philippines of the Kalayaan Islands".[15]

In a letter to Marcos on 22 March 1972, a former Philippine diplomat, Juan Arreglado, signing himself as "Chairman Advisory Council of the Free Territory of Freedomland", complained that "the claims now put forward by the Philippine Government run counter to its formal commitments as expressly stated in the letter" of Secretary García of 8 February 1957. Arreglado claimed that the exchange of letters between Cloma and García made clear the Philippines' "recognition of the existence of the Free Territory of Freedomland as a 'Protected State'" of the Philippines. Quoting Ingles as saying at the UN that "Freedomland ... has been and is now under effective occupation and control of the Philippine Government", Arreglado stated that the undersecretary had indicated a change in the official position of the Philippines "by laying claim directly to ownership and occupation of Freedomland".[16]

This internal Philippine dispute seems to have been resolved by the "Deed of Assignment and Waiver of Rights" that Cloma, on behalf of Tomás Cloma & Associates, signed on 4 December 1974 transferring to the Philippine Government "all rights and interests they might have acquired" over "Freedomland" on the strength of "discovery and occupation" and by virtue of "exploration, development, exploitation, and utilization". The deed reproduced the coordinates laid down in the original proclamation and charter, both dated 6 July 1956.[17]

However, the deed was apparently executed under duress. In their biography of Cloma, José V. Abueva, Arnold P. Alamon and Oliva Z. Domingo write:

> The Philippines' subsequent claim to Freedomland since 1974 is based on Cloma's involuntary cession of his rights to the Government under the martial law regime of President Marcos.... In December 1974, the

Government forcibly took over Freedomland from Cloma and Associates while Cloma was still under house arrest after spending 57 days in prison at Camp Crame, the headquarters of the Philippine Constabulary in Quezon City... . Under extreme duress, (Cloma, then 70) had to cede all the rights over Freedomland acquired by Cloma and Associates to the Philippine Government.... His daughter, Celia, convinced him to finally cede his rights over Freedomland/Kalayaan Islands in exchange for his freedom.[18]

In a 15 July 1987 memorandum addressed to President Corazon C. Aquino, Arreglado and Pedro Vargas, writing for Tomás Cloma & Associates, asked for the reimbursement of "expenses" incurred from 1947 to 1974 in the "exploration, occupation, development, administration, organization and settlement of Freedomland". The memorandum charged that "the arrest and detention of Atty. Tomas Cloma, Sr. was motivated solely by the overwhelming desire of the Martial Law Regime ... to induce and compel Tomas Cloma & Associates to accept and sign the ... Deed of Assignment and Waiver of Rights...." It claimed that, "in view of the fact that Atty. Tomas Cloma, Sr. was already more than seventy years of age at that time, with frail physical constitution and whose health required then medical care and attention, and the threat hanging over his head that he would be rearrested and detained again in the stockade for an indefinite period of time, Tomas Cloma & Associates had no other alternative but to agree and sign the aforesaid DEED."[19]

Then, Tomás Cloma & Associates stated that, "despite all the acts of injustice, compulsion and abuse of power inflicted on the person of Atty. Tomas Cloma, Sr. by the ruling authorities of the Martial Law Regime, we are in perfect accord with the issuance on June 11, 1978 of Presidential Decree No. 1596" claiming possession of and sovereignty over "Freedomland". After setting forth the bases and reasons for its claim to "Freedomland" and describing its background, Tomás Cloma & Associates requested 50 million Philippine pesos from the Philippine government as "just, equitable and reasonable" compensation for laying the basis for "the eventual acquisition of ownership and sovereignty over Freedomland by the Philippines."[20] Thus, despite the charge that Cloma had signed under duress the transfer of all rights to and interests in "Freedomland" to the Philippine government in 1974, Tomás Cloma & Associates was now, in 1987, freely affirming that transfer.

On 11 June 1978, under his martial-law powers, Marcos had issued a decree formalizing the Philippine claim, declaring that an area off Palawan outside the Treaty of Paris limits, "including the seabed, subsoil, continental margin and air space", was to "belong and be subject to the sovereignty of the Philippines". To be known as "Kalayaan", meaning freedom, the area was almost entirely congruent with but slightly larger than Cloma's "Freedomland". The decree, numbered PD 1596, designated, both in the preamble and in the operative part, the coordinates bounding the claimed area:

> From a point [on the Philippine Treaty Limits] at latitude 7°40' North and longitude 116°00 East of Greenwich, thence, due West along the parallel of 7°40' N to its intersection with the meridian of longitude 112°10' E, thence, due north along the meridian of 112°10' E to its intersection with the parallel of 9°00' N, thence northeastward to the intersection of parallel of 12°00' N with the meridian of longitude 114°30' E, thence, due East along the parallel of 12°00' N to its intersection with the meridian of 118°00' E, thence, due South along the meridian of longitude 118°00' E to its intersection with the parallel of 10°00' N, thence Southwestwards to the point of beginning at 7°40' N, latitude and 116°00' E longitude.

The area thus claimed covered 70,150 square nautical miles (see Figure 2).

The decree constituted Kalayaan "as a distinct and separate municipality of the Province of Palawan". It asserted that "much of the ... area is part of the continental margin of the Philippine archipelago" and that "by virtue of their proximity" the island group was "vital to the security and economic survival of the Philippines". It invoked "history, indispensable need, and effective occupation and control established in accordance with international law" in supporting the Philippine claim, affirming that other states' "claims to some of these areas ... have lapsed by abandonment". Since then, the residents of the islands occupied by the Philippines, including the troops there, have taken part in Philippine elections. By June 1978, Philippine forces had occupied four more islands or other land features, in addition to the three whose occupation Marcos had announced in July 1971. Afterwards, the Philippines is reported to have taken possession of two more land features in the Spratlys.

Although it is outside the limits set by the Treaty of Paris and other international agreements governing Philippine territory, the Philippines considers Scarborough Shoal, a group of islands, reefs and rocks in the South China Sea about 200 kilometers west of Subic Bay in Luzon, as part of the main Philippine archipelago. It has been the scene of much Philippine activity. For centuries, Filipino fishermen have used its waters for fishing and its lagoon for shelter. When the United States was still in control of large military bases in the Philippines, the United States, as well as the Philippine, Air Force used Scarborough for target practice. Media reports state that the Philippines constructed a lighthouse and raised its flag on the shoal in the 1960s. The Philippine Navy has operated in the area and occasionally arrested or chased away foreign fishermen, particularly those engaged in illegal fishing methods. Scarborough's official Philippine name, Bajo de Masinloc, meaning "below Masinloc" in Spanish, refers to Masinloc, a town in Zambales province, the Spanish-language name of Scarborough obviously dating it back to Spanish times.

In November 2007, Representative Antonio V. Cuenco of Cebu filed a bill in the House of Representatives seeking further to amend the baselines act of 1961, as amended in 1968. In doing so, the bill would extend the Philippines' baselines to connect the outermost points of the area in the South China Sea claimed in the 1978 Marcos decree and in the Scarborough Shoal area. There would be twelve such points in the Kalayaan Island Group and six at Scarborough Shoal. The bill prescribed that, in the case of each of two base points in Kalayaan, Iroquois Reef and Sabina Shoal, a "permanent structure such as a lighthouse should be established on its low-tide elevation".[21] This suggestion was obviously motivated by the need to have the proposed base points conform to the UNCLOS requirements on such base points and the baselines that connect them.

Evidently with the UNCLOS requirements and foreign policy and tactical considerations in mind, however, the Department of Foreign Affairs opposed the move to draw the baselines to encompass the entire Kalayaan claim and Scarborough Shoal. President Gloria Macapagal-Arroyo, in January 2009, endorsed a version introduced in the Senate by three of its committees and six individual senators, including Miriam Defensor-Santiago. Supported by the Department of Foreign Affairs, the Senate bill would *not* extend the baselines to the Kalayaan Island Group or Scarborough Shoal. Instead, it would declare a "regime of islands", as envisioned in Article 121 of the UNCLOS, for the land features in the Kalayaan Island Group as defined in the Marcos decree and Bajo de Masinloc, that is, Scarborough Shoal.[22] The Senate version substantially prevailed in the bill that the Congress finally passed and President Arroyo signed into law on 10 March 2009.[23]

The new act invokes Article 121 of the UNCLOS in declaring a "regime of islands" for the land features in the Philippine-claimed Kalayaan Island Group and Scarborough Shoal. According to that article, an island may have its own territorial sea, contiguous zone, exclusive economic zone and continental shelf as determined in the same way as other land territory. However, "(r)ocks which cannot sustain human habitation or economic life of their own shall have no exclusive economic zone or continental shelf". The Philippines has refrained from designating which of the South China Sea land features that it claims are islands and which are mere "rocks" in the UNCLOS sense, apparently preferring to reserve for itself a measure of ambiguity. Moreover, the Philippines retains the option of amending the new law in the future so as to draw baselines around the Kalayaan islands or Scarborough Shoal or both. Nevertheless, by maintaining its baselines only around its main archipelago, instead of using Scarborough shoal and other land features in the South China Sea as base points, and declaring a regime of islands for those features, the new law brings the Philippine claim closer to conformity with the UNCLOS as far as the maritime regimes in these areas are concerned. This is something that still cannot be said of the Chinese or Vietnamese claim. China and Vietnam promptly lodged protests against the enactment of the new law, asserting their claims to both the Spratlys and Scarborough Shoal. Unfortunately, some commentators confuse the original Cuenco bill, which would have extended the Philippines' archipelagic baselines to the Spratlys and Scarborough Shoal, with the act as finally passed and signed into law, which does not.

CHINA'S CLAIM

Partly in response to the Cloma group's activities, Taiwanese forces, in July 1956, returned to re-establish a permanent presence on Itu Aba. After the Japanese defeat in the Pacific War, those forces had planted Nationalist Chinese flags and stone markers on Itu Aba, Spratly Island and West York Island and set up a garrison on Itu Aba in December 1946, mainly to forestall apparent French attempts to return to the area. Moreover, the Allies had designated the (Nationalist) Chinese as recipients of the surrender of the Japanese forces in the area north of 16° North latitude. However, the Nationalists abandoned Itu Aba in June 1950, evidently for two reasons. One was the fall of the southern Chinese island of Hainan to the Communist Chinese, which made it difficult for the Nationalists to supply the garrison on Itu Aba. The other reason was that all Nationalist forces were deemed necessary for the defence of Taiwan itself.

On 7 July 1956, Cloma and several Philippine Maritime Institute cadets delivered to the (Nationalist) Chinese embassy in Manila a Nationalist Chinese flag that Cloma said they had removed from Itu Aba. The removal of the flag had evoked a protest from the Nationalist Chinese government. At the beginning of October, as the institute's training ship lay at anchor in the northwest corner of the area claimed by Cloma, it was approached by two Nationalist Chinese naval vessels. Filemon Cloma, Tomás Cloma's younger brother, who was in command of the Philippine ship, was invited to board one of the Nationalist Chinese vessels, where a heated four-hour discussion of the islands' ownership took place. During this time, a "Chinese boarding party" searched the PMI ship and confiscated arms, maps and documents. Hartendorp's citation of Tomás Cloma's account continues:

> The next day, the Captain was again invited aboard the Chinese ship, and this time he took two of his officers with him and was treated "more formally." But "even under grave threats to their lives, Captain Cloma refused to sign a statement that they will leave Freedomland and will not come back. He also refused to recognize that Freedomland is Chinese territory. However, he was forced to accede to surrender the arms against receipt."[24]

Lu Ning, a Chinese academic who used to be an official at the Chinese Foreign Ministry, cites a different version of those events. Quoting Taiwan's "An Account of Naval Patrol in the Spratly Sea Frontiers", he states that the (Nationalist) Chinese "obtained" from Captain Cloma the following note, which the Chinese had evidently written for him:

> We assure that we received your friendly visit and check with no disturbance or anything lost on board of our ship. In order to keep up sincere friendship between the Republic of China and the Republic of the Philippines, we will not make further training voyages or landings in the territorial waters of your country and will accept your proper disposal after investigations in conformity with national laws of the Republic of China and international law in case we break our promise.[25]

China claims that it has long considered the Spratlys, as well as the Paracels, as its own, calling the Spratlys and environs Nan Sha and the Paracels area Xi Sha. The Chinese claim, espoused by both Beijing and Taipei, which basically have the same outlook on territorial issues, goes all the way back to the Han Dynasty (206 BC to 220 AD) and invokes sporadic contacts by Chinese people with the islands of the South China Sea, as reflected in travel reports, classical literature and local chronicles. Also cited have been the maps drawn in the Tang Dynasty (618–907) and the standardization of the islands' names and descriptions of currents in the Song (960–1279). So have been the establishment of an astronomical observation point in the Spratlys by the Yuan Dynasty (1271–1368) and the identification of the South China Sea islands in records of the Zheng He voyages during the Ming period (1368–1644). The more or less permanent presence of Hainanese fishermen in the South China Sea islands from as early as the Jin Dynasty (265–420) to the twentieth century has been noted.

As international acceptance of the Western concept of jurisdiction over fixed territories gained momentum, China — imperial, Nationalist and the People's Republic — took actions to assert its claim to the South China Sea islands in contemporary ways, like official statements, protests, the reaffirmation of claims, maps, agreements and conventions, laws, and various other acts of sovereignty. These often took the form of protests against the claims and encroachments of others while asserting Chinese ownership of and sovereignty over the islands and, ambiguously, the seas around them. In 1883, the Chinese protested against German surveys of the Paracels and the Spratlys. As a result of China's defeat by France in a war over French designs on Vietnam, the Chinese were compelled in 1887 to sign a treaty that, among other provisions, apparently assigned the Paracels and the Spratlys to China. To pre-empt further French moves and thwart French ambitions, China sent in 1902 a naval task force to inspect the South China Sea islands, planting flags and markers there. In 1907, as an outcome of another inspection tour, detailed plans were drawn up for the exploration of resources in and around the islands. In 1911, the new republic that had replaced the Qing Dynasty (1644–1911) placed the Paracels and the Spratlys under a county on Hainan. In December 1947, even as the Chinese civil war was going on, the Chinese communists incorporated the two groups of islands into Guangdong province. [26]

In 1947, the Nationalist government of China published a map, the Location Map of the South China Sea Islands, in which nine bars or an "interrupted line" enclosed the South China Sea. The U-shaped series of bars starts, on the north, between Luzon and Taiwan, skirts the western coast of Luzon and Palawan and East Malaysia, and, from 4°N latitude, rises northwards along the eastern coast of Vietnam. It remains unclear what those nine bars signify — whether they represent a Chinese claim to all the waters within them, a claim that would contravene the UNCLOS, which does not recognise "historical" claims to open seas, or merely to the land features that they encompass and the maritime regimes that those features generate.

Sam Bateman, a Senior Fellow at the S. Rajaratnam School of International Studies of the Nanyang Technological University in Singapore and a former Australian naval officer, asserts that it cannot be the former, since the bars are merely drawn on a map without the coordinates required for establishing jurisdictional boundaries. [27] B. A. Hamzah of the University of Malaya, formerly with the Maritime Institute of Malaysia and Malaysia's Institute of Strategic and International Studies, agrees that "without the coordinates the line is not legal", only showing China's "dominion or suzerainty" in the South China Sea. He points out that, the nine bars having antedated the UNCLOS's coming into force, no Chinese political leaders would be willing to drop the line lest they be accused of abandoning China's historical claim to the South China Sea. "Nevertheless," Hamzah stresses, "it will indeed be a gesture of goodwill to take steps to make the line consistent with UNCLOS."[28] In any case, ASEAN delegations have asked Chinese officials directly what the nine bars indicate, but have not elicited a definitive response. It is interesting to note that Indonesia, concerned over a possible Chinese claim to its gas-rich Natuna archipelago, has put the query down in writing.

Although China was not a participant in the 1951 San Francisco conference, Zhou Enlai, then foreign minister of the People's Republic of China, issued a statement before the treaty of peace with Japan was signed asserting Chinese sovereignty over the Spratlys and the Paracels. The new government in Beijing had hit out at a U.S.-U.K. draft for the treaty. The draft, eventually adopted in substance, declared that Japan was renouncing all claims to the Paracels and the Spratlys but did not specify which party would have sovereignty over them. (A Soviet attempt to declare Chinese ownership of and sovereignty over the islands had been soundly voted down.) A similar provision was included in the 1952 Japan-(Nationalist) China treaty of peace. Although the provision also failed to state to which party the Paracels and Spratlys belonged, Lu Ning argues:

> The Sino-Japanese Treaty is different from the San Francisco Treaty in two ways. The former is a bilateral treaty, dealing with only bilateral issues. The intended recipient for the territories, though not mentioned, is obvious. Secondly, unlike the San Francisco Treaty which treats the Paracels and the Spratlys in a separate paragraph from the one dealing with Taiwan and the Pescadores, the Sino-Japanese Treaty includes them in one single paragraph, thus indicating that Japan considers the legal status of the South China Sea archipelagos the same as those of Taiwan and the Pescadores.[29]

In September 1958, the People's Republic of China issued a Declaration on the Territorial Sea. That document extended the breadth of China's territorial sea to 12 nautical miles, a concept that had been gaining currency in international discussions on maritime issues and was to be finally enshrined in the 1982 UNCLOS. The declaration, at that time still using the Wade-Giles system of English orthography, applied the extension "to all territories of the People's Republic of China, including the Chinese mainland and its coastal islands, as well as Taiwan and its surrounding islands, the Penghu (Pescadores) Islands, the Tungsha Islands, the Hsisha Islands (Paracels), the Chungsha Islands (Macclesfield Bank), the Nansha Islands (Spratlys) and all other islands belonging to China which are separated from the mainland and its coastal islands by the high seas".[30] The designation of the waters between the mainland and the claimed island possessions as "the high seas" could be interpreted as ruling out the notion that the Chinese considered the entire South China Sea as territorial or internal waters.

In 1988, China created a new province, called Hainan, out of Hainan island, the Paracels, Macclesfield Bank and the Spratlys, all of which, according to Chinese law, had belonged to Guangdong Province. In February 1992, the Standing Committee of China's National People's Congress passed a law proclaiming the country's 12-nautical mile territorial sea and a contiguous zone with a breadth of 12 nautical miles beyond the territorial sea, as the UNCLOS prescribes. Its Article 2 states, using *pinyin* in the English translation, "The PRC's territorial sea refers to the waters adjacent to its territorial land. The PRC's territorial land includes the mainland and its offshore islands, Taiwan and the various affiliated islands including Diaoyu Island, Penghu Islands, Dongsha Islands, Xisha Islands, Nansha (Spratly) Islands and other islands that belong to the People's Republic of China."[31] Although the law reaffirms China's claim to the land features in the South China Sea as its "territorial land", it does not make the distinction between islands, which, under the UNCLOS, can generate their own territorial sea, contiguous zone and exclusive economic zone, and mere rocks, which cannot. The nature of the maritime regimes around those land features thus remains unclear and ambiguous.

VIETNAM'S CLAIM

From the late 1920s to shortly after World War II, the French, too, actively maintained a claim to the Spratlys, a claim that Vietnam was to press as its own in its capacity as successor-state to France. A June 1929 letter from the governor of Cochinchina, in today's Vietnam, indicated that Spratly Island had been "administratively joined" to Baria province. In April 1930, the French raised their flag on Spratly Island, and their Indochinese authorities announced the island's annexation. Three years later, they sent vessels to the Spratlys and occupied six islands there, publishing in July 1933 an official notice of their annexation and, later in the year, declaring them as part of Baria province, an act that the Republic of Vietnam confirmed in 1956. Claiming the islands as theirs, the Chinese protested the 1933 French actions. So did the Japanese, who started in late 1937 to occupy some of the islands in the Spratlys. In 1939, the Japanese declared their occupation of the Pratas, the Paracels and the Spratlys, placed the Spratlys, which they named Shinnan Gunto (New Southern Archipelago), under the administration of Kaohsiung on Taiwan, then a Japanese colony, and later used them to launch attacks on Southeast Asia. The British, too, who were also claiming Spratly Island and Amboyna Cay, had protested against the French claims and actions in the Spratlys.

Like the Chinese, the Vietnamese date their presence in the Paracels and the Spratlys to centuries past and lay claim to them on the basis of discovery, use and occupation. At the 1951 San Francisco Peace Conference, the Vietnamese representative, Tran Van Huu, Prime Minister and Minister of Foreign Affairs, asserted Vietnam's right to the Paracels and the Spratlys, without anyone challenging him. As recalled above, South Vietnam protested against Cloma's announcement of his "discovery" of "Freedomland". It affirmed Vietnam's ownership of the Spratlys as successor-state to France, which, however, having annexed the islands in the 1930s, claimed continued sovereignty over the archipelago.

After the 1954 Geneva agreements resulted in the temporary partition of Vietnam, South Vietnam took over about half of the Paracels from the French, who had laid claim to them, as they did to the Spratlys, in the early 1930s. The forces of the People's Republic of China, on the other hand, had maintained their hold on Woody Island and other parts of the eastern portion of the Paracels, having taken them from the Nationalists. Nationalist forces had gone to that part of the Paracels to receive the surrender of Japanese troops in pursuance of the 1945 Potsdam Proclamation. In September 1973, South Vietnam, after awarding offshore oil-exploration contracts to leading multinational companies, announced the annexation of eleven land features in the Spratlys.

Within about four months, in January 1974, Chinese and South Vietnamese naval and commando forces clashed in the Paracels as they pursued their countries' conflicting claims to the entire area. In the end, the Chinese troops evicted the South Vietnamese from the Paracels. The Chinese thus avoided the necessity of seizing the islands from a reunified Vietnam ruled by China's then allies in Hanoi, which was closely linked to the power of the Soviet Union, a source of threat to Beijing. With the Paris negotiations on a political settlement of the Vietnam conflict going on, the United States, for its part, refrained from going to the aid of its South Vietnamese allies.

The retreating South Vietnamese forces repaired to the Spratlys. In April 1975, even before the fall of Saigon, North Vietnamese forces forcibly took the land features occupied by the South Vietnamese in the Spratlys. By 1987, Vietnam had occupied fifteen land features in the Spratlys. With the Chinese attack on Vietnam towards the end of 1978 having brought the animosity between the two countries out into the open, and with Soviet military support for Vietnam now unlikely, Chinese forces engaged those of Vietnam near Johnson Reef in the Spratlys area in March 1988. The brief naval battle resulted in more than seventy Vietnamese dead and one Vietnamese vessel sunk and two damaged. In geopolitical terms, the more serious outcome was that their victory in that battle enabled the Chinese to firm up and expand their military presence in the Spratlys. In June 1988, they set up their first permanent military post there, and two months later conducted military exercises around the islands, reefs and atolls. In April and May 1989, they occupied two more atolls in the Spratlys previously held by Vietnam.[32] At the same time, Vietnam increased the number of land features under its control to twenty-one in 1988 and to twenty-four in 1989. On the other hand, by 2000, China had occupied seven land features in the Spratlys, not including the Taiwanese-occupied Itu Aba.

MALAYSIA AND BRUNEI DARUSSALAM

In October 1977, Malaysia placed sovereignty markers on eleven land features in the Spratlys and, in December 1979, published a new map depicting its territorial waters and continental shelf. The continental shelf and exclusive economic zone projected from East Malaysia, that is, from Sabah and Sarawak, encompassed the southern portion of the Spratlys, which is part of the areas claimed by China, Vietnam and the Philippines and covered the continental shelf and "exclusive fishing zone" of Brunei Darussalam. Notably, the Malaysian claim includes Amboyna Cay, where Vietnam is present by virtue of a previous French claim, and Commodore Reef (Terumbu Laksamana), which the Philippines occupies (and calls Rizal Reef). In 1983, Malaysia proceeded to establish a permanent presence on Terumbu Layang-Layang (Swallow Reef), which it opened for tourism in 1991. The Malaysians have also occupied Terumbu Ubi (Ardasier and Dallas Reefs), Terumbu Mantanani (Mariveles Reef), and Terumbu Peninjau (Investigator Reef). Malaysia bases its claim on the features' location on its continental shelf and has invoked national security and their proximity to the Malaysian mainland in making the claim.

Since 1984, Brunei Darussalam has claimed an "exclusive fishing zone" and a continental shelf projected from its coastline into the South China Sea. Brunei Darussalam and Malaysia have been holding talks, at least since 2003, on their conflicting claims. At the end of the visit to Brunei Darussalam of Malaysia's then-Prime Minister Abdullah Ahmad Badawi on 15–16 March 2009, the Malaysian leader and Brunei's Sultan Hassanal Bolkiah issued a joint press statement announcing, among other things:

> Both Leaders noted the agreement of their respective Governments on the key elements contained in the Exchange of Letters, which included the final delimitation of maritime boundaries between Brunei Darussalam and Malaysia, the establishment of Commercial Arrangement Area (CAA) in

oil and gas, the modalities for the final demarcation of the land boundary between Brunei Darussalam and Malaysia and unsuspendable rights of maritime access for nationals and residents of Malaysia across Brunei's maritime zones en route to and from their destination in Sarawak, Malaysia provided that Brunei's laws and regulations are observed.[33]

The texts of the letters exchanged have not been made public, but on 3 May 2010 Malaysia's Ministry of Foreign Affairs issued a statement on the 16 March 2009 agreement. The statement read in part:

> The key elements are the final delimitation of maritime boundaries between Malaysia and Brunei Darussalam, the establishment of a Commercial Arrangement Area (CAA) for oil and gas, the modalities for the final demarcation of the land boundary between Malaysia and Brunei Darussalam, and unsuspendable rights of maritime access for nationals and residents of Malaysia across Brunei Darussalam's maritime zones.

> With regard to the maritime areas, the Exchange of Letters established the final delimitation of territorial sea, continental shelf and exclusive economic zone of both States. Malaysia's oil concession Blocks L and M which coincided with Brunei Darussalam's Blocks J and K are recognised under the Exchange of Letters as being situated within Brunei Darussalam's maritime areas, over which Brunei Darussalam is entitled to exercise sovereign rights under the relevant provisions of the United Nations Convention on the Law of the Sea 1982 (UNCLOS 1982). The establishment of the CAA incorporating these Blocks provides for a sharing of revenues from the exploitation of oil and gas in the CAA between the two States.[34]

The statement said that the Malaysian Cabinet had approved the contents of the agreement. The land boundary mentioned by both the March 2009 joint statement and the May 2010 foreign ministry statement refers to Limbang, a part of Malaysia's Sarawak that separates the two parts of Brunei Darussalam.

After he stepped down from Malaysia's political leadership, Abdullah Badawi, on 30 April 2010, had explained on the Malaysian foreign ministry's website:

> Regarding the maritime area, Malaysia and Brunei also agreed to establish a final and permanent sea boundary. This agreement serves to settle certain overlapping claims which existed in the past, which included the area of the concession blocks known before as Block L and Block M. Sovereign rights to the resources in this area now belongs to Brunei. However for this area, the agreement includes a commercial arrangement under which Malaysia will be allowed to participate on a commercial basis to jointly develop the

oil and gas resources in this area for a period of 40 years. The financial and operational modalities for giving effect to this arrangement will be further discussed by the two sides. This means that in so far as the oil and gas resources are concerned, the agreement is not a loss for Malaysia.[35]

UNCLOS AS WATERSHED

One way of considering the conflicting claims to the waters of the South China Sea would be to use the effectivity of the UNCLOS as a kind of historical watershed, with agreed rules governing such claims after the UNCLOS entered into force for its signatories. All claimants to the South China Sea are parties to the convention. The Philippines was the eleventh party to ratify it, in 1984. Vietnam followed ten years later. China, Malaysia and Brunei Darussalam did so in 1996. Before the UNCLOS's entry into force on 16 November 1994, the nature of the maritime regimes that China, Vietnam and the Philippines were claiming was vague at best. Lu Ning has pointed out that, up to at least the Ming Dynasty (1368–1644), the Chinese concept of jurisdiction was based on the "nationality principle" rather than on "well-defined geographical territory". China seems to have begun accepting, in some measure, Western concepts of geographic international boundaries by the late seventeenth century and, specifically, maritime boundaries by the late nineteenth century. Lu Ning goes on:

> Furthermore, the concept of geographically-based sovereignty with rigidly delineated territorial land and waters in which the state exercises exclusive jurisdiction was alien to China and much of the rest of Asia. For centuries China had maintained an elaborate hierarchical system of a universal state in which the central empire oversaw a hierarchy of tributary states. Jurisdiction was based on social organization, history, degree of sinicization and the loyalty of subjects. Consequently, Chinese boundaries in the periphery were never carefully delineated in accordance with contemporary international law and tended to be ill-defined and vague. What are regarded as official acts of territorial acquisition in contemporary international law, such as raising the flag and making official proclamations of incorporation, were neither known to nor necessary for China which regarded itself as the centre of a universal state that answered to no one.[36]

The Chinese concept of a "hierarchical system of a universal state" has, of course, become obsolete, even, it seems, in the Chinese view, as it has become accepted that international relations are based on well-defined territorial jurisdictions. With respect to maritime jurisdictions, the UNCLOS and previous maritime agreements lay down specific rules and criteria for determining the nature and extent of regimes on the sea and on the seabed, although, even after the ratification and entry into force of the UNCLOS, some claims continue to be vague and sea-related rules continue to be the subject of conflicting interpretations. Almost all countries of the world have ratified the UNCLOS, the most egregious exception being the United States. They include most, if not all, of Asia, counting even such land-locked countries as Laos and Mongolia. Thus, without going into the legal niceties and nuances of this matter, one could say that all claimants to waters of the South China Sea have to ensure that their claims are based on and consistent with the provisions of the UNCLOS, to which they are all parties, notwithstanding the fact that some of those provisions remain open to different interpretations. At the same time, one must remember that the UNCLOS does not deal with the substance of claims to land features or their bases, in the South China Sea or elsewhere. As a Taiwan scholar has been quoted as pointing out, "it is not the waters which give title to islands but islands which confer rights to waters".[37]

With the Philippines in early 2009 declaring a regime of islands for Scarborough Shoal and the other land features in the South China Sea that it claims, it has moved in the direction of making its claims more consistent with the UNCLOS. Malaysia and Vietnam seem to have done so, too. On 6 May 2009, Malaysia and Vietnam filed, as required by the UNCLOS, a "joint submission" to the UN Commission on the Limits of the Continental Shelf, which, according to Robert Beckman, Director of the Centre for International Law and associate professor of law at the National University of Singapore, "suggests that they have taken the position that sovereign rights to the resources of the South China Sea should be determined by principles governing the continental shelf as measured from the mainland coast." Beckman continues, "By not measuring their continental shelves or EEZs from any of the islands which they claim in the South China Sea, they have in effect taken the position that no islands in the South China Sea should be entitled to more than a 12nm territorial sea — the maximum permitted by UNCLOS."[38]

Thus, with Malaysia and Brunei Darussalam appearing to have negotiated a settlement of their overlapping maritime claims, the Southeast Asian claimants seem to have made their respective claims more closely aligned with the pertinent UNCLOS provisions. China, on the other hand, while maintaining the official character of the nine bars, has not defined the nature of the waters that they encompass.

The Southeast Asian claimants' moves have, of course, not completely clarified the kinds of maritime regime envisioned in their claims. Much less have the basic conflicts among the various claims to land features been resolved. As long as the claims to the land features, to the islands, reefs, shoals and atolls, remain in conflict, the claims to the waters around them cannot be reconciled. In this situation, the most that the claimants can do is to reassure one another that they will not resort to military force to assert their claims and not occupy hitherto unoccupied features. They can adopt other confidence-building measures and carry out cooperative activities, including joint development. One step towards mutual confidence could be to clarify the nature of one's maritime claims in the South China Sea and to align those claims, as far as possible, with the provisions of the UNCLOS.

DEALING WITH CHINA

China, of course, is uppermost in the concerns of the Philippines, as well as of other Southeast Asian countries, with respect to the South China Sea. The Philippines has regarded China, among the rival claimants to the Spratlys, as the only source of military threat and as the only potential hegemon in the region. It certainly cannot match China in military power. The Philippines has also known that it cannot depend on its 1951 mutual defence treaty with the United States or, until 1992, when the Philippine-U.S. military bases agreement expired, on the presence of those bases as a deterrent to any Chinese threat in the South China Sea. After all, the United States has repeatedly made it known that it does not consider the mutual defence treaty to apply to the disputed territories in the South China Sea, although the United States has expressed its opposition to the use of force in asserting claims there and to attempts to exercise hegemony in the region. At the same time, the Chinese have made repeated assurances that they would respect freedom of navigation in the South China Sea, a matter of primary concern to the United States. In this light, Manila has relied on strengthening relations with China and, after the discovery of Chinese facilities on Mischief Reef, on raising the political and diplomatic cost of any change, Chinese-induced or otherwise, to the status quo in the South China Sea. Its hold on those land features that it claims and occupies has been made more tenacious. Part of this has been the putative strengthening of the legal basis for the Philippine claim to Scarborough Shoal and the Kalayaan Island Group.

The need to deal with the jurisdictional disputes in the South China Sea and their strategic implications was one of the three principal motives for Manila's decision, in the early 1970s, to extend recognition to the People's Republic as the government of all of China, transfer diplomatic relations from Taipei to Beijing, and otherwise establish good relations with the communist regime. (The other two were to seal Beijing's commitment to cease its support for the communist insurgency in the Philippines and to seek assurances, in a period of energy insecurity, of the supply of Chinese crude oil, at "friendship prices", at a time when China was still an exporter of oil.)

In the talks during the breakthrough visit of President Ferdinand Marcos to China in June 1975, the last year of the Great Proletarian Cultural Revolution, Deng Xiaoping, newly rehabilitated (only to be sacked again ten months later) and subbing as Vice Premier for the ailing Premier Zhou Enlai, proposed that the issue of sovereignty pertaining to the South China Sea be "shelved" and that the two countries embark on "joint development" in the area, a proposal that Deng and his successors have repeated to Vice President Salvador Laurel, President Corazon Aquino and other Philippine leaders and, at every opportunity, to others in the world ever since.

Five months after the publication in February 1992 of China's law on its territorial sea and contiguous zone, referred to above, which re-affirmed Beijing's claim to the land features of the South China Sea, the Philippines chaired and hosted the ASEAN Ministerial Meeting and Post-Ministerial Conferences, the annual gatherings of the foreign ministers of ASEAN and its Dialogue Partners. Manila took the opportunity to lead ASEAN in issuing, on 22 July, the ASEAN Declaration on the South China Sea. The declaration affirmed that "sovereignty and jurisdictional issues" were to be resolved "by peaceful means, without resort to force". It urged "all parties concerned to exercise restraint". The ministers would "explore the possibility of cooperation" on the safety of maritime navigation and communication, the protection of the marine environment, search-and-rescue operations, combating piracy and armed robbery at sea, and the campaign against illicit trafficking in drugs. Finally, the declaration called for the application of the principles of the Treaty of Amity and Cooperation in Southeast Asia as a basis for a "code of international conduct over the South China Sea".[39]

The foreign ministers of China and Russia, ASEAN's "consultative partners", attended the public sessions as guests of the ASEAN chairman. Raul Manglapus, the Philippines' Secretary of Foreign Affairs, and Romualdo Ong, the country's representative to the ASEAN Senior Officials Meeting, sought to get China to associate itself with the declaration. After hurried telephone consultations with Beijing, Qian Qichen, the Chinese foreign minister, declined the proposal on the ground that China had not been involved in the drafting of the resolution. Perhaps a deeper and more genuine reason was the Chinese preference for bilateral discussions on the South China Sea issues to dealing with ASEAN as a group. However, he said, China associated itself with the declaration's "principles".

In February 1995, the atmosphere of sweetness and light generated by the steadily strengthening relationship of China with ASEAN and its members was rudely disturbed by the discovery of Chinese structures on Mischief Reef, a mostly underwater reef in the South China Sea just a little over 200 kilometers west of the Philippine island of Palawan. (Its English name is attributed to Heribert Mischief, a German member of the crew of Henry Spratly, who is said to have discovered the reef in 1791. China calls it Meiji Jiao, and the Philippines Panganiban Reef.) The Philippine government apparently learned about the Chinese occupation when several Filipino fishermen reported that Chinese on the reef had detained them for over a week. Photographed by the Philippine Air Force, the structures appeared to be made of steel, flew the Chinese flag, and displayed quite clearly parabolic antennas on their roofs. The Chinese initially claimed, however, that these were intended as shelters for Chinese fishermen. It took all of two weeks for the Chinese foreign ministry to react to the Philippines' announcement of its discovery. As for ASEAN, on 18 March 1995, a few weeks after the announcement, the foreign ministers issued a statement entitled "Recent Developments in the South China Sea (1995)" and saying, in full:

> We, the ASEAN Foreign Ministers, express our serious concern over recent developments which affect peace and stability in the South China Sea.
>
> We urge all concerned to remain faithful to the letter and spirit of the Manila Declaration on the South China Sea which we issued in July 1992 and which has been endorsed by other countries and the Non-Aligned Movement. The Manila Declaration urges all concerned to resolve differences in the South China Sea by peaceful means and to refrain from taking actions that de-stabilize the situation.
>
> We call upon all parties to refrain from taking actions that destabilize the region and further threaten the peace and security of the South China Sea. We specifically call for the early resolution of the problems caused by recent developments in Mischief Reef.
>
> We urge countries in the region to undertake cooperative activities which increase trust and confidence and promote stability in the area.
>
> We encourage all claimants and other countries in Southeast Asia to address the issue in various fora, including the Indonesia-sponsored Workshop Series on Managing Potential Conflicts in the South China Sea.[40]

The strong, if non-hostile, tone of this statement reflected the alarm with which the ASEAN senior officials viewed the Mischief Reef developments. Although the statement did not mention China by name, the reference was clear. Indeed, in the process of discussing these developments and drafting the ASEAN statement on them, the senior officials were clearly concerned by China's possible intention and its temerity in extending its sway all the way to Mischief Reef.

At the first meeting of the ASEAN and Chinese senior foreign ministry officials, in April 1995 in Hangzhou, a forum that I had proposed the year before, the ASEAN delegations raised pointed questions about the Chinese position on the South China Sea and particularly about the developments on Mischief Reef. The ASEAN officials, including those whose countries laid no claims to any part of the South China Sea, also asked the Chinese directly about the significance of the nine bars enclosing the entire South China Sea on Chinese maps without eliciting a response. (The Chinese have not responded either to the same, but more formal, query that Indonesia had addressed to them, although they are said to have assured Indonesia that there was "no problem" between the two countries concerning territorial or maritime claims.) Nevertheless, the discussions were significant, being the first time that China dealt with the South China Sea question in a multilateral setting, as opposed to its preference for discussing it only bilaterally.

In the same month, Secretary of Foreign Affairs Roberto R. Romulo, testifying before a joint hearing by the House Committees on Foreign Affairs and Defense on the developments on Mischief Reef, laid down the elements of the Philippine position on the issue:

- The Panganiban Reef is part of Philippine territory. As sovereign owners, we will enforce our laws....
- The actions taken by elements identified with the People's Republic of China are violative of international law and the norms of friendly relations between nations.
- The Philippines will exhaust all peaceful means in resolving this issue....
- While the use of self-defense is our inherent right, the aggressive use of force is not an option.
- This matter is not just a bilateral concern for the Philippines, but a multilateral concern for all claimants and all other parties interested in the peace and stability of the region.[41]

At their annual meeting in July, the ASEAN foreign ministers stated in their joint communiqué:

The Foreign Ministers expressed their concern over recent events in the South China Sea. They encouraged all parties concerned to reaffirm their commitment to the principles contained in the 1992 ASEAN Declaration on the South China Sea, which urges all claimants to resolve their differences by peaceful means and to exercise self-restraint. They also called on them to refrain from taking actions that could destabilise the region, including possibly undermining the freedom of navigation and aviation in the affected areas. They also encouraged the claimants to address the issue in various bilateral and multilateral fora.[42]

In August, as Undersecretary of Foreign Affairs of the Philippines, I held talks in Manila with Wang Yingfan, then the Director-General of the Department of Asian Affairs of China's Ministry of Foreign Affairs, in which we discussed the Mischief Reef issue. We agreed that, pending the resolution of the dispute, the two sides would refrain from using force and instead seek to settle their disputes peacefully through consultations, "in accordance with the recognized principles of international law, including the UN Convention on the Law of the Sea", and "without prejudice to the freedom of navigation in the South China Sea". We also agreed that our countries would promote cooperation in a wide range of areas, including "the protection and conservation of the marine resources of the South China Sea".[43]

The next year, in March, I had another round of consultations with China, also in Manila, this time with Tang Jiaxuan, Vice Minister of Foreign Affairs and later foreign minister and then State Councilor. Re-affirming the provisions of the August 1995 joint statement, we agreed to set up "a bilateral consultative mechanism to explore ways of cooperation in the South China Sea".[44]

In May 1996, China announced the baselines along its southeastern coast and around the Paracels. These are straight baselines connecting forty-nine base points, identified by coordinates, along the coast and linking twenty-eight base points, also defined by precise coordinates, around the Paracels. A number of scholars have pointed out that China could not legally draw straight baselines around the Paracels, as that group of islands cannot be considered as an archipelago under the UNCLOS. Some have even questioned the way the baselines were drawn. The Chinese declaration also stated, "The Government of the People's Republic of China will announce the remaining baselines of the territorial sea of the People's Republic of China at another time."[45] Significantly, no baselines have been announced since then for the Spratlys or for any other area in the South China Sea outside the Paracels.

THE DECLARATION ON THE CONDUCT OF PARTIES

At every opportunity, the Philippines and ASEAN as a whole have sought to "internationalize" the South China Sea issue so as to subject the Chinese to greater international pressure. ASEAN has endeavoured to draw international attention to the South China Sea as a flashpoint for regional tension and conflict and a possible threat to maritime shipping, including at the United Nations, forums like the ASEAN-EU Ministerial Meeting, and, starting at the 1992 NAM summit chaired and hosted by Indonesia, the meetings of the Non-Aligned Movement (NAM). (All ASEAN members belong to NAM, which China attends, although it is not a member.) The Philippines has also emphasized the environmentally destructive — and illegal — methods of fishing, like dynamite and cyanide, used by Chinese — and Taiwanese — as well as other, fishermen in waters under Philippine jurisdiction, disputed or not.

At the first ministerial meeting of the ASEAN Regional Forum (ARF), in July 1994, the South China Sea issue had, in deference to Chinese sensitivities, been discussed not in plenary but over dinner. At the very next meeting, in August 1995, after the revelation of China's occupation of Mischief Reef, the subject moved to the regular session. According to the chairman's statement of that meeting, the ministers "expressed concern on overlapping sovereignty claims in the region. They encouraged all claimants to reaffirm their commitment to the principles contained in relevant international laws and convention, and the ASEAN's 1992 Declaration on the South China Sea".[46] Discussions on the subject, however, became more and more perfunctory, as ASEAN and China undertook negotiations on a code of conduct for the South China Sea and as the realization dawned on the participants that the ARF was not built to resolve questions of territorial jurisdiction or otherwise do anything concrete about them.

Following the discovery of the Chinese installations on Mischief Reef, the Philippines sought to engage China in the development of an agreed code of conduct for the South China Sea in order to reduce the sense of threat and uncertainty among countries and peoples concerned with the area. The process involved the rest of ASEAN as a group. While ASEAN gained by the apparent willingness of China to speak to ASEAN as an entity, it lost in terms of the waning interest on the part of the rest of the international community in the issue.

In the joint communiqué issued at the end of their annual meeting in July 1996, the ASEAN foreign ministers stated:

> The Foreign Ministers expressed their concern over the situation in the South China Sea, and stressed that several outstanding issues remain a major concern for ASEAN. In the spirit of the Manila Declaration on the South China Sea, the Ministers called for the peaceful resolution of the

dispute and self-restraint by parties concerned. The Ministers were pleased to observe, however, that the parties concerned have expressed their willingness to resolve the problem by peaceful means in accordance with recognized international law in general and the UNCLOS of 1982 in particular. The Ministers also reiterated the significance of the on-going informal workshop series on Managing Potential Conflict in the South China Sea, and welcomed the continuing bilateral cooperation and discussions among the claimant countries. They endorsed the idea of concluding a regional code of conduct in the South China Sea which will lay the foundation for long-term stability in the area and foster understanding among claimant countries. (Typographical errors have been corrected.)[47]

In the negotiations on a code of conduct that followed, China adamantly refused to include the Paracels in the scope of the code. As expected, Vietnam was the strongest advocate of their inclusion. The failure to agree on the area coverage of the instrument led to the refusal of some of the negotiators to accept calling it a "code", which, it was argued, would imply its legally binding character, something impossible to do without a clear definition of where it would apply. Thus, the document finally adopted was called the "Declaration on the Conduct of Parties in the South China Sea". The ASEAN foreign ministers and Wang Yi, China's Vice Foreign Minister designated as Special Envoy for the event, signed the declaration in Phnom Penh on 4 November 2002 on the occasion of the annual ASEAN-China Summit.

The declaration committed the ASEAN countries and China to freedom of navigation and overflight in the South China Sea, the peaceful settlement of disputes there, and the exercise of "self-restraint", specifically refraining from inhabiting "presently uninhabited" land features. They undertook to promote mutual confidence through, among other means, dialogues between defence and military officials, the "just and humane treatment" of persons in danger or in distress, the voluntary prior notification of joint or combined military exercises, and the voluntary exchange of "relevant information". They agreed to cooperate in a wide range of areas, including marine environmental protection, marine scientific research, the safety of navigation and communication at sea, search and rescue, and combating transnational crime. However, the declaration did not specify the deployment of military forces or the reinforcement of structures in already occupied land features among the activities to be covered by self-restraint.[48]

In September 2004, during a hurried visit by President Arroyo to China, among the agreements signed in her presence was an "Agreement for Seismic Undertaking for Certain Areas in the South China Sea By and Between China

National Offshore Oil Corporation and Philippine National Oil Company". Although the text of the agreement was not made public, the Philippine government did explain in a press release that PNOC and CNOOC would do a joint seismic study in the South China Sea for three years, denying, to rather universal disbelief, that the agreement had any "reference to petroleum exploration and production" and adding that "the national *oil* (italics mine) company of a third country" could take part. The agreement surprised and upset other ASEAN countries, primarily Vietnam. In March 2005, however, Vietnam, probably seeing the futility of opposing it, joined in the arrangement, which was duly modified. The Chinese, who conducted most of the survey, are reported not to have shared all of their findings with the Philippines or Vietnam. Barry Wain, writer-in-residence at the Institute of Southeast Asian Studies in Singapore and formerly of the *Wall Street Journal Asia*, wrote in early 2008:

> For a start, the Philippine government has broken ranks with the Association of Southeast Asian Nations, which was dealing with China as a bloc on the South China Sea issue. The Philippines has also made breathtaking concessions in agreeing to the area for study, including parts of its own continental shelf not even claimed by China and Vietnam. Through its actions, Manila has given a certain legitimacy to China's legally spurious "historic claim" to most of the South China Sea....
>
> Ironically, it was Manila that first sought a united front and rallied Asean to confront China over its intrusion into Mischief Reef a decade earlier. Sold the idea by politicians with business links who have other deals going with the Chinese, Ms. Arroyo did not seek the view of her foreign ministry, Philippine officials say.[49]

The article raised an uproar in political circles and in the mass media in the Philippines, although the agreement in question had been concluded more than three years before. The agreement was allowed to expire in June 2008.

While the Philippines-China deal marked, as an unintended consequence, a departure from the multilateral approach that Manila had sought to foster in dealing with China with respect to the South China Sea, the Philippines apparently did not enter into the agreement within a broad strategic context. After all, neither the Department of Foreign Affairs nor the National Security Council had been involved in, much less consulted on, it; only the national oil company ostensibly took part. In any case, the agreement's expiration seems to have laid the matter to rest, except that Manila's willingness to conclude it may have raised doubts about the Philippines' dependability on this and other issues.

Although the Chinese have retreated in some measure and resigned themselves to dealing with ASEAN as a group, they seem to have maintained their old position of insisting on holding bilateral discussions with individual Southeast Asian claimants. In a lecture at the Institute of Southeast Asian Studies organized by ISEAS' ASEAN Studies Centre in November 2009, China's ambassador to ASEAN, Xue Hanqin, declared:

> In the follow-up negotiations on the draft guidelines for the implementation of the DOC (Declaration on the Conduct of Parties in the South China Sea), the work got stuck mainly because of the difference over the modality of their (ASEAN member-states') consultations. The key issue is whether ASEAN Member States should consult among themselves first before they consult with China. ASEAN members insist on such a consensual approach towards China, while the Chinese side does not think this is in line with the understanding of DOC... . The whole issue of South China Sea is not a matter between ASEAN as an organization and China, but among the relevant countries. ASEAN could serve as a valuable facilitator to promote mutual trust among the Parties, but not turn itself into a party to the dispute.[50]

In this regard, one must make the distinction between the negotiation or adjudication of the legal jurisdictional disputes and the interim measures that must be taken in managing the situation created by the disputes. In negotiating a territorial dispute or submitting it for adjudication, only the parties to the dispute are and should be involved. Even here, in the case of the Spratlys, the process of negotiation or adjudication is made extremely complicated by the fact that more than two parties are involved. On the other hand, in terms of the measures for managing the situation pending a settlement of the jurisdictional issues, clearly all ASEAN member countries, and others affected, have an interest in them. All have a stake in regional peace, in the relaxation of regional tensions, in the promotion of stability in the area, in cooperation in ensuring the cleanliness and productivity of a shared body of water, and in keeping trade routes and transportation links open and free. The DOC was negotiated between ASEAN and China. The declaration was issued on the occasion of the ASEAN-China summit. All ASEAN member states participated in its negotiation and are parties to it. At bottom, no outside party can or should tell ASEAN on what issues its members are to take coordinated or common positions.

Recently, however, the Chinese seem to have come around to emphasizing the need to distinguish between negotiating or adjudicating the jurisdictional or sovereignty disputes, in which only the parties concerned should be involved, and what they call "confidence-building" measures, in which a much larger number of countries have an interest.

THE U.S. INVOLVEMENT

The United States created a stir in July 2010, when, at the annual ministerial meeting of the ASEAN Regional Forum (ARF), Secretary of State Hillary Rodham Clinton reiterated, in unusually clear and strong terms, the American position on the South China Sea disputes and its interest in that body of water. What she actually said at the meeting has apparently not been made public. However, the U.S. Department of State has released the transcript of the media conference that Secretary Clinton gave immediately after the ARF meeting. The transcript quotes her as saying:

> The United States supports a collaborative diplomatic process by all claimants for resolving the various territorial disputes without coercion. We oppose the use or threat of force by any claimant. While the United States does not take sides on the competing territorial disputes over land features in the South China Sea, we believe claimants should pursue their territorial claims … and rights to maritime space in accordance with the UN convention on the law of the sea. Consistent with customary international law, legitimate claims to maritime space in the South China Sea should be derived solely from legitimate claims to land features.
>
> The US supports the 2002 ASEAN-China declaration on the conduct of parties in the South China Sea. We encourage the parties to reach agreement on a full code of conduct. The US is prepared to facilitate initiatives and confidence building measures consistent with the declaration because it is in the interest of all claimants and the broader international community for unimpeded commerce to proceed under lawful conditions. Respect for the interests of the international community and responsible efforts to address these unresolved claims and (sic) help create the conditions for resolution of the disputes and a lowering of regional tensions.[51]

At the ARF ministerial meeting, China's foreign minister, Yang Jiechi, almost immediately responded to Secretary Clinton's statement. The text of his remarks has not been made public either, but the website of China's Ministry of Foreign Affairs gives a detailed account of what he said:

> Yang said, the first question is what is the situation in the South China Sea. Is it peaceful and stable? Or is it tense? From today's discussion, most people say the situation is peaceful. And in my bilateral discussions with both ASEAN colleagues and others, they all say that there is no threat to regional peace and stability.

Second, is it an issue between China and ASEAN as a whole? Obviously not. We do have some territorial or maritime rights disputes with certain members of ASEAN. It is because we are neighbors. And those disputes shouldn't be viewed as ones between China and ASEAN as a whole just because the countries involved are ASEAN members. The non-claimant ASEAN countries tell the Chinese side that they are not part of the disputes, they don't take sides and they hope these disputes will be settled through bilateral consultations between the countries concerned.

Third, what is the consensus of countries in the region with regard to the South China Sea issue? The consensus is to have these disputes solved peacefully through friendly consultations in the interest of peace and stability in the South China Sea and good-neighborly relations. According to the *Declaration on the Conduct of Parties in the South China Sea* (DOC), it is to exercise restraint, and not to make it an international issue or multilateral issue. Channels of discussion are there, and they are open and smooth. Everybody admit this.

Fourth, what is the function of the DOC? Its function is to enhance mutual trust among the countries concerned and to create favorable conditions and good atmosphere for final solution to the disputes. China and ASEAN countries issued this DOC. There have been joint working group consultations. And when the conditions are ripe, senior officials' meeting can also be held.

Fifth, has navigation freedom and safety been hindered in the South China Sea? Obviously not. Trade has been growing rapidly in this region and China has become the number one trading partner of many countries in the region. Some countries have not been able to export more to China, not because the navigation freedom has been hindered, but because they set high barriers for high-tech exports.

Sixth, what is the purpose of talking about coercion on the South China Sea issue? China all along believes that all countries, big or small, are equal. China, being a big country, also has its legitimate concerns. Is the expression of one's legitimate concerns coercion? That is not logical. The non-claimant countries hate it that some try to coerce them into taking sides on the South China Sea issue.

Seventh, what will be the consequences to if this issue is turned into an international or multilateral one? It will only make matters worse and the resolution more difficult. International practices show that the best way to resolve such disputes is for countries concerned to have direct bilateral negotiations. Asia has already stood up and gained its dignity. Asian countries can properly address each other's concerns on the basis of equality and mutual respect.[52]

THE POSSIBILITY OF RESOLUTION

It is highly unlikely that the jurisdictional disputes in the South China Sea will be resolved anytime soon, if ever. If only bilateral issues were involved, they could in theory be resolved by recourse to the International Court of Justice in The Hague, by arbitration, or by other peaceful means of settling international disputes. Even so, the litigation would be fraught with difficulty and uncertainty. In the case of the Spratlys, the multilateral character of the disputes and the varied natures of the claims make the conflicting claims immensely more complex. There is, of course, the possibility of the use of armed force. A successful resort to force could entrench the dominance of the power wielding it, but, under present and foreseeable circumstances, would not resolve the disputes themselves to the satisfaction of all. It could result only from a particularly unfortunate concatenation of massive political and strategic miscalculations and only make things worse. Hence, neither armed conflict nor a definitive legal resolution is likely or plausible in the South China Sea in the foreseeable future.

Most fundamentally, the resolution of the jurisdictional disputes is possible only as a result of a combination of compromises worked out by the claimant states. However, such compromises are made extremely difficult, if not impossible, first, by the nationalist emotions — and the tendency of politicians to exploit or be swayed by them — inevitably aroused by territorial issues. Related to this is the aversion of political leaders to appearing to be giving up national territory or other areas of jurisdiction.

Secondly, and perhaps more importantly, the claimants consider their positions on and in the South China Sea as vital to their strategic interests. Malaysia has to have some degree of control over the vast expanse of sea that separates — and connects — East and West Malaysia. Brunei Darussalam seeks to secure for itself jurisdiction over its exclusive economic zone and continental shelf, which cuts right across Malaysia's claimed EEZ, and the right to exploit the resources in them. The Philippines would feel threatened from the west if it did not push out the frontiers of its jurisdiction to its claimed Kalayaan Island Group and Scarborough Shoal. China seeks control of the South China Sea in order to avoid being "contained", pressured or even attacked from the southeast, as it was in the past, and to increase Beijing's influence on an important passageway for international trade. When it was in authority over China, the Nationalists were driven by the same motives. Today, although now confined to the islands that they control, Taiwan politicians cannot be seen as being weaker than Beijing in asserting territorial claims. Refusing to leave China in control of what it calls the East Sea, Vietnam would be hemmed in by Chinese power if it did not have a foothold on the South China Sea.

Non-claimants, too, have a deep interest in peace and stability in the region of the South China Sea and in freedom of navigation on and overflight over that body of water. Included in these are countries whose international trade traverses the South China Sea in large volumes, countries like those of ASEAN, Japan, South Korea, Taiwan, Hong Kong, Europe's leading trading nations, the United States and China itself. The exporters of crude oil, much of their products destined for East Asia, also have a stake in what happens in the South China Sea. The United States professes an interest in the right to ferret out information on military developments in China on the grounds of the alleged lack of transparency in those developments, a right that Beijing, of course, contests.

On a global scale, the clash of interests that seems to have the greatest impact on the world in general and on Southeast Asia in particular is the one between the interests of China, which considers the South China Sea issue as primarily for the claimants to deal with, and those of the United States, which insists on its role as vital to Asia-Pacific peace and stability and on its interest in freedom of navigation on and overflight over the world's oceans. Yet, the interests of China and the United States are so intertwined politically and economically in Asia and around the world that both have a stake in good and stable relations between them. Southeast Asia, too, including the Philippines, has an interest in the well-being and stability of those bilateral, great-power relations. At the same time, there seems to be a contradiction between, on the one hand, the desirability of the United States lending its powerful voice to the rule of international law and to free and open sea and air lanes and, on the other, the proposition that public pressure can only harden Chinese disregard for the UNCLOS's strictures on maritime claims. It was probably with the latter in mind that the Philippines' foreign secretary, Alberto Romulo, declined, as reported by Agence France-Presse, to support publicly Hillary Clinton's ARF intervention.

Meanwhile, there remain problems that can be dealt with and opportunities that can be seized only through international cooperation, primarily among the claimants. Sam Bateman observes:

> Most regional analysts agree that conflict between the parties is most unlikely. However, there is a need to acknowledge that sovereignty claims, and hence maritime boundaries, will not be resolved in the foreseeable future. We must get away from the notion that the South China Sea can be managed effectively on the basis of unilateral jurisdiction and sole ownership of the resources. A cooperative management regime is the only solution.
>
> The only acceptable framework for such a regime would appear to be a web of provisional arrangements covering cooperation for different functions

and perhaps even with different geographical areas for each function. The functions to be considered might include development of oil and gas resources, fisheries management, marine safety, law and order at sea, marine scientific research, and preservation and protection of the marine environment. However, such an approach requires a lot of talking, bargaining and some "give and take". This is not occurring at present.[53]

Despite the reasonableness of his proposition, Bateman himself acknowledges that "negotiating a joint arrangement between three or more parties can prove extremely difficult".[54] One difficulty is the lack of confidence and mutual suspicion between the claimants, a condition exacerbated by the very existence of the conflicting claims. Another is that many attempts at or proposals for cooperation would run into questions of sovereign jurisdiction.

In the case of the Philippines, its current constitution provides, "The State shall protect the nation's marine wealth in its archipelagic waters, territorial sea, and exclusive economic zone, and reserve its use and enjoyment exclusively to Filipino citizens."[55] Unless some way is found to get around this constitutional constraint, it would be difficult for the Philippines to conduct "joint development" of the resources in its maritime jurisdiction, particularly since Manila has refrained from identifying which of the land features that it claims are islands and which are mere rocks; thus, its maritime jurisdiction in the Spratlys and the area of application of the constitutional constraint cited above remain murky.

Much has been made and written about the energy resources beneath the South China Sea and the fish that abound in it as critical reasons, in an era of concern over energy and food scarcity, for the scramble for jurisdiction over the land features and seas of that body of water. The recent history of the Spratlys has been marked by claimants granting to international companies oil and/or gas concessions in areas of the South China Sea that they claim, which then provokes protests from other claimants. However, just as fundamental, and often related to the need for secure access to the food and energy resources of the South China Sea, are the claimants' strategic considerations, described above.

Driven by such considerations, none of the claimants can afford to back down from its claims to the land features of the South China Sea. In the interest of regional peace and stability, the most that one can expect in the foreseeable future is far from a definitive resolution of the conflicting claims — a "grand solution", in the words of Mark Valencia, a leading authority on maritime issues. Even attempts to adjust the maritime claims to the requirements of the UNCLOS, as the Philippines, Vietnam, Malaysia and

Brunei Darussalam seem to have made in early 2009, can be considered as endeavours to strengthen the legal foundations of the claims. Nevertheless, declaring a regime of islands for the claimed land features in the South China Sea on the part of China and Vietnam could make the maritime regimes around those features less ambiguous and thus constitute a step towards a further relaxation of tensions in the area.

Meanwhile, in order to reduce the chances of territorial disputes developing into armed conflict, measures could be taken to increase the claimants' stakes in good relations with one another and in cooperation for common purposes and to raise the political cost of any resort to violent action. In this light, one can place one's hopes on the reluctance of any of the claimants, at this point, to upset the regional stability from which all of them have benefited so much, provided that no one is given cause to perceive any immediate threat to its core interests. The same holds true for the United States as well as China.

THE INFORMAL WORKSHOPS

It is to build mutual confidence, overcome mutual suspicions and work out mutually beneficial cooperative activities, while promoting the principle of non-recourse to force or other unilateral action, that Hashim Djalal, Indonesia's foremost authority on maritime law, has spearheaded the series of "Workshops on Managing Potential Conflict in the South China Sea". Convened by Indonesia's Department of Foreign Affairs and Centre for Southeast Asian Studies, the annual workshops, all held in one place or another in Indonesia, started in 1990 and, until 2001, were supported by the Canadian International Development Agency through the University of British Columbia. Participants in the workshops include officials, in their "personal capacity", from all ASEAN countries, claimants or not, and, significantly, since 1991, from both the Chinese mainland and Taiwan, as well as Vietnam (which was to become an ASEAN member only in 1995).

In the pursuit of confidence building, "joint development" and networking, the workshops promote peaceful cooperative activities. Specifically, these activities cover assessments of living and non-living resources, marine environmental protection, navigational safety, search and rescue, and marine scientific research. For these purposes, a working group on marine scientific research deals with the development of a database and the exchange of information, the monitoring of the sea level and tides, and biodiversity. There is a technical working group on the environment. The technical working group on legal matters stays away from questions of jurisdiction but addresses less controversial issues like drug trafficking, piracy, armed robbery at sea, environmental legislation, the interpretation of the UNCLOS, and legal issues arising from the work of other groups.[56]

Although the workshops are not meant to resolve or even discuss jurisdictional issues, they do build confidence, promote the exercise of self-restraint, uphold the principle of the non-use of force in dealing with territorial questions, provide a venue for dialogue, consultation and the clarification of issues, and foster cooperation. It was at the workshops that the Philippines and China first discussed the elements of a code to govern conduct in the South China Sea.

The 2001 workshop was the last one that Canada supported. The participants, nevertheless, decided to convene the workshop the next year and to contribute to the series' funding on a voluntary basis. The workshop has taken place every year since then.

To skirt the problem of jurisdiction, Hashim Djalal for a while pushed the idea of cooperation in an area in the middle of the South China Sea where no exclusive economic zone, legitimately measured and projected from mainland or archipelagic baselines, overlaps with another (dubbed the "doughnut" scheme). The proposal, however, apparently has not gained traction, although a Chinese scholar seems to have revived it recently even if Beijing had initially opposed it.

CONCLUSION

In the conclusion to their paper on the South China Sea, Clive Schofield and Ian Storey point out that, in the end, it will take a political settlement to resolve the South China Sea disputes, the prospects of which are exceedingly slight:

> Diplomacy is still the favored option by all parties concerned, and there remains a general commitment to cooperative approaches aimed at reducing the chances of conflict, joint development, and protecting the marine environment. Yet the political will to translate rhetoric into reality is lacking as demonstrated by the failure of ASEAN and China to conclude a more robust Code of Conduct for the South China Sea. All the while, the claimants continue to build up their presence in the Paracel and Spratly Islands, fortify their occupied atolls, and enhance their military capabilities.

> In the end, for all the merits of exhaustive analyses of the relative virtues (or otherwise) of each claimant state's territorial and maritime claims in international legal terms, it has to be recognized that this would only really be relevant were the disputes to be resolved through international adjudication and this remains a remote possibility. This is not to argue that

the legal positions of the parties are not important and will not influence negotiating positions or be subject to lively debate and contention among the parties, but it is nonetheless clear that if the South China Sea disputes are to be settled, such resolution will derive from a political rather than essentially legal process. Unfortunately, the prospects of such a political settlement seem vanishingly small.[57]

While Schofield and Storey are right in their assessment, policy-makers in the claimant countries need to move towards improving the situation, even if such moves are short of a definitive settlement of their conflicting claims, the prospects of which, in any case, are, in the words of Schofield and Storey, "vanishingly small".

One such move would be to improve on the current Declaration of Conduct. Schofield and Storey call for a "more robust" code of conduct, Hillary Clinton for a "full" code of conduct. Others have been more specific, envisioning a code of conduct that is "legally binding". In such visions, it is unclear who would enforce the code and how. This means that there would really be no substantive difference between a legal code and a political declaration. Moreover, until the question of whether it would cover the Paracels is resolved, no "legally binding" code is possible, unless the parties change their positions, the irreconcilable nature of which made the adoption of a "legally binding" code impossible in the first place. Instead, ASEAN and China would do well to build and put flesh on the current declaration by carrying out its provisions, elaborating on them or taking measures not foreseen in it but consistent with its spirit.

The first principle of the declaration is the peaceful settlement of disputes. This means that not only must the settlement of disputes be peaceful, that is, not by force, but moves have to be made towards a settlement. For one thing, China has to stop proclaiming that it has "indisputable sovereignty" over the South China Sea, when there are, in fact, disputes, which are the source of the problem to begin with. The claimants should begin to distinguish among the land features that they claim which are islands and which are rocks, as defined by Article 121 of the UNCLOS. This distinction is critical to the kinds of maritime jurisdiction that one can claim. Making it can bring a measure of clarity to the claimants' maritime claims and to the rights of others and thus, particularly if done simultaneously, improve stability in the region.

The declaration enjoins the exercise of "self-restraint" on the parties, specifically committing them to "refraining from action of inhabiting on (sic) the presently uninhabited islands, reefs, shoals, cays, and other features". The parties could agree to specify that the deployment of military forces or the reinforcement of structures in already occupied land features is among the activities covered by self-restraint.

The declaration calls for dialogues and exchanges of views between their defence and military officials as a confidence-building measure. In October 2010, the defence ministers of ASEAN's ten members and eight other countries, including China, Japan and the United States, met for the first time in Hanoi. As reported in the media, among the wide range of subjects discussed — among the eighteen and in bilateral talks — was the situation in the South China Sea. In this sense, one of the measures that the declaration calls for is already being carried out. Subsequent meetings, too, could offer opportunities for the ministers of China and other claimant-countries to hold confidence-building talks.

The parties to the declaration might enter into specific agreements committing them to carrying out the measures specified in it, including "ensuring just and humane treatment" of persons "in danger or in distress", notifying "other Parties concerned" of impending joint or combined military exercises, and exchanging "relevant information". They could undertake the cooperative activities that the declaration suggests in the areas of the marine environment, marine scientific research, safety of navigation, search and rescue, and combating transnational crime.

Above all, aligning claims with the provisions and requirements of the UNCLOS would go a long way towards reducing mutual suspicions, stabilising things in East Asia, ensuring open and free sea lanes and aviation paths, helping to improve relations all around, and, for the Philippines, the diminution of a sense of threat to the national security.

Notes

1. Republic of Vietnam Ministry of Foreign Affairs, *White Paper on the Hoang Sa (Paracel) and Truong Sa (Spratly) Islands* (Saigon, 1975), p. 75.
2. A. V. H. Hartendorp, *History of Industry and Trade of the Philippines: The Magsaysay Administration* (Manila: Philippine Education Company, 1961), p. 212.
3. The text of the Notice is in Appendix D to Juan M. Arreglado, *Kalayaan: Historical, Legal, Political Background* (Manila: Foreign Service Institute, 1982), p. 21.
4. Quoted in Hartendorp, *History of Industry and Trade*, p. 212.
5. Quoted in ibid., p. 213.
6. These documents are reproduced as Appendices E, F, G, H, I, K and L to Arreglado, *Kalayaan*, pp. 22-34.
7. Quoted in Hartendorp, *History of Industry and Trade*, pp. 223–24.
8. Ibid., p. 225.

9. Republic of Vietnam Ministry of Foreign Affairs, *White Paper*, p. 75.

10. Ibid., p. 231.

11. Quoted in full in Hartendorp, *History of Industry and Trade*, pp. 232–33.

12. The Spratlys take their name from Richard Spratly, a British whaler of the nineteenth century.

13. Appendix S to Arreglado, *Kalayaan*, pp. 45–46.

14. Appendix R to Arreglado, *Kalayaan*, pp. 43–44.

15. José D. Ingles, *Philippine Foreign Policy* (Manila: Lyceum of the Philippines, 1982), p. 229.

16. Appendix P to Arreglado, *Kalayaan*, pp. 39–41.

17. Appendix Z to Arreglado, *Kalayaan*, pp. 83–84.

18. José V. Abueva, Arnold P. Alamon and Oliva Z. Domingo, *Admiral Tomas Cloma* (Quezon City, Philippines, University of the Philippines, 1999), pp. 33–34, 51 and 151.

19. Tomás Cloma & Associates, *Memorandum for Her Excellency Corazon C. Aquino, President of the Philippines, Malacañang Palace, Manila* (15 July 1987), document in author's possession.

20. Ibid.

21. Text of House bill in author's possession.

22. Text of Senate bill in author's possession.

23. Rodolfo C. Severino, *Clarifying the New Philippine Baselines Law* (Singapore: Online Discussion Forum, ASEAN Studies Centre, Institute of Southeast Asian Studies, <www.iseas.edu.sg/aseanstudiescentre>, 2009).

24. Hartendorp, *History of Industry and Trade*, pp. 224–27.

25. Lu Ning, *Flashpoint Spratlys!* (Singapore: Dolphin Trade Press Pte Ltd, 1995), p. 32.

26. The Chinese claim is summarized in ibid., pp. 5–30.

27. Sam Bateman, *Commentary on "Energy and Geopolitics in the South China Sea" by Michael Richardson* (Singapore: Online Discussion Forum, ASEAN Studies Centre, Institute of Southeast Asian Studies, <www.iseas.edu,sg/aseanstudiescentre>, 2009), pp. 7–8.

28. B. A. Hamzah, *Pax Sinica and Regional Maritime Order in the Spratlys* (Singapore: Online Discussion Forum, ASEAN Studies Centre, Institute of Southeast Asian Studies, <www.iseas.edu.sg/aseanstudiescentre>, 2009), p. 4.

29. Lu Ning, *Flashpoint Spratlys!*, p. 30.

30. An English translation of the declaration is appended to Jeanette Greenfield, *China and the Law of the Sea, Air, and Environment* (Germantown, Maryland, USA: Sijthoff and Noordhoff, 1979), p. 243.

31. http://huwu.org/Depts/los/LEGISLATIONANDTREATIES/PDFFILES/CHN_1992_Law.pdf.

32. This narrative is taken from Bob Catley and Makmur Keliat, *Spratlys: The Dispute in the South China Sea* (Aldershot, England, and Brookfield, Vermont, USA: Ashgate Publishing, 1997), p. 82. That account, in turn, is based on contemporary media reports.

33. <http://www.fmprc.gov.cn/ce/cebn/eng/wlxw/t542877.htm>, para. 3.

34. <http://www.kln.gov.my/web/guest/pr2010/-/asset_publisher/X9Nx/content/
press-release-:-the-exchange-of-letters-between-yab-dato'-seri-abdullah-haji-
ahmad-badawi-prime-minister-of-malaysia-and-his-majesty-sultan-haji-hassanal-
bolkiah-mu'izzaddin-waddaulah-english-version-only;jsessionid=868CDC42196
5796C4269F388022C0C81?redirect=%2Fweb%2Fguest%2Fpr2010>.

35. Statement by Tun Abdullah Ahmad Badawi on the Exchange of Letters Between
Malaysia and Brunei Darussalam, dated 16 March 2009 (<http://www.kln.gov.
my/web/guest/>).

36. Lu Ning, *Flashpoint Spratlys!*, p. 16.

37. Steven Yu Kuan-tsyh, "Who Owns the Paracels and Spratlys? An Evaluation of the
Nature and Legal Basis of the Conflicting Territorial Claims", paper presented at
the second Workshop on Managing Potential Conflicts in the South China Sea,
Bandung, Indonesia, 15–18 July 1991, p. 27, as quoted in Catley and Keliat,
Spratlys, pp. 38–39.

38. Robert Beckman, "South China Sea: Worsening Dispute or Growing Clarity in
Claims?", in *RSIS Commentaries* (Singapore: S. Rajaratnam School of International
Studies, 16 August 2010), p. 2.

39. <http://www.asean.org/3634.htm>.

40. <http://www.asean.org/5232.htm>.

41. Roberto R. Romulo, *The Tasks Before Us: Territorial Integrity and Regional Peace
and Stability* (Manila, 10 April 1995).

42. Joint Communique of the Twenty-Eighth Asean Ministerial Meeting, Bandar Seri
Begawan, 29–30 July 1995 <http://www.aseansec.org/2087.htm>, para. 9.

43. Joint Statement: RP-PRC Consultations on the South China Sea and on Other
Areas of Cooperation, 9–10 August 1995.

44. Joint Press Communiqué on Philippines-China Consultations, 15 March
1996.

45. Declaration of the Government of the People's Republic of China on the
baselines of the territorial sea, 15 May 1996 <http://www.un.org/Depts/los/
LEGISLATIONANDTREATIES/PDFFILES/ CHN_1996_Declaration.
pdf>.

46. <http://www.aseanregionalforum.org/PublicLibrary/ARFChairmans
StatementsandReports/ChairmansStatementofthe2ndMeetingoftheASE/
tabid/199/Default.aspx>.

47. Joint Communique of The 29th ASEAN Ministerial Meeting (AMM) Jakarta,
20–21 July 1996 <http://www.asean.org/3663.htm>, para. 11.

48. <http://www.aseansec.org/13163.htm>.

49. Barry Wain, "Manila's Bungle in the South China Sea", *Far Eastern Economic
Review*, January/February 2008.

50. Xue Hanqin: *China-ASEAN Cooperation: A Model of Good Neighbourliness and
Friendly Cooperation*, Singapore, 19 November 2009 <http://www.iseas.edu.
sg/aseanstudiescentre/Speech-Xue-Hanqin-19-9-09.pdf>, pp. 24–25.

51. Remarks at Press Availability by Secretary Hillary Rodham Clinton in Hanoi,

Vietnam, 23 July 2010, in <http://www.state.gov/secretary/rm/2010/07/145095.htm>.

52. Foreign Minister Yang Jiechi Refutes Fallacies on the South China Sea Issue <http://www.mfa.gov.cn/eng/zxxx/t719460.htm>.

53. Sam Bateman, *Commentary*, p. 8.

54. Ibid., p. 8.

55. Section 2, Article XII, of the 1987 Philippine Constitution.

56. The statements issued at the end of the 1991 to 2002 workshops are reproduced in Hasjim Djalal, *Preventive Diplomacy in Southeast Asia: Lessons Learned* (Jakarta: The Habibie Center, 2003), pp. 229–78.

57. Clive Schofield and Ian Storey, *The South China Sea Dispute: Increasing Stakes and Rising Tensions* (Washington, D.C.: The Jamestown Foundation, November 2009), p. 42.

6

PHILIPPINE MARITIME JURISDICTION AND UNCLOS

On 11 November 1967, Arvid Pardo, Malta's permanent representative to the United Nations, delivered a lengthy presentation to the First Committee (political and security) of the UN General Assembly. In that presentation, Malta, a small island nation in the Mediterranean, proposed "an effective international regime over the seabed and the ocean floor beyond a clearly defined national jurisdiction (through which) all can receive assurance that at least the deep sea floor will be used exclusively for peaceful purposes and that there will be orderly exploitation of its resources". He called for "a special agency with adequate powers to administer in the interests of mankind the oceans and the ocean floor beyond national jurisdiction".[1]

What worried Pardo and Malta most were three trends. One was the rapid development of technology to mine the ocean floor and the soil beneath it, which were outside both national jurisdiction and international control. The combination of technological development and the anarchical state of the oceans, the seabed and its subsoil would cause the gap between the technologically advanced and the rest of the world to widen even more. Another trend was the growing capacity of ever-larger oil tankers and other vessels to pollute the seas and of fishing fleets operating at long distances to deplete fishery resources. The third was the possibility of a militarily advanced nation placing weaponry on the seabed and negating its adversary's second-strike nuclear capability, the core of nuclear deterrence during the Cold War. This would endanger the planet and everyone on it.

This state of near-anarchy arose from the fact that the oceans beyond a narrow band of sea along the coastlines of states, together with their resources in the waters, on the seabed and in its subsoil, were free for use, exploitation or despoliation by others. Shortly after the end of World War II, in September 1945, the United States laid claim to ownership of the natural resources on its continental shelf, "subject to its jurisdiction and control". Argentina then extended that to include the sea above the continental shelf. Soon afterwards, alarmed by the potential depletion of their fish stocks through the activities of fishing fleets from other continents, several coastal states in Africa led by Kenya and in South America — Chile, Peru and Ecuador, to begin with — asserted their economic rights over a 200-mile maritime zone off their coasts. At the same time, several countries extended the breadth of their territorial seas to twelve miles from the traditional three miles.

Indonesia and the Philippines claimed sovereignty over the waters around and between their islands in accordance with the "archipelagic doctrine", still undefined with any precision at the time, arousing the concern of shipping nations. Moreover, in 1949, the Philippines had laid claim to petroleum and natural gas in "submerged lands within the territorial waters or on the continental shelf, ... seaward from the shores of the Philippines which are not within the territories of other countries," as belonging to the state.[2] The Philippines had also been insisting that all "water areas embraced within the lines described in the Treaty of Paris" of 1898, the U.S.-Spain treaty of 1900, the U.S.-United Kingdom agreement of 1930, and the U.S.-U.K. Convention of July 1932 "are considered as maritime territorial waters of the Philippines for purposes of protection of its fishing rights, conservation of its fishery resources, enforcement of its revenue and anti-smuggling laws, defence and security, and protection of such other interests as the Philippines may deem vital to its national welfare and security, without prejudice to the exercise by friendly foreign vessels of the right of innocent passage over those waters".[3]

It was in this situation of gathering international turmoil that the Third Conference on the Law of the Sea convened in 1973, six years after Malta's historic proposal. To be sure, there were two previous attempts to bring some kind of order out of this growing chaos. The First Conference on the Law of the Sea, in Geneva in 1958, resulted in four conventions — on the territorial sea and contiguous zone, on the continental shelf, on the high seas, and on fishing and conservation of living resources of the high seas. David D. Caron, professor of law at the University of California, Berkeley, has pointed out:

> The results of the conference were splintered into four separate Conventions. A state could sign as many or as few of them as it wished, defeating the intention of creating a comprehensive governance scheme. Because the Conventions combined customary international law with new international

law, if a state opted not to sign all the Conventions, there was uncertainty as to the international norms applicable to that party. The possibility of a new consensus emerging as a result of the conference also had not taken into account the large number of states that would be decolonization (sic) in the years after the conference, states which had not participated in the negotiations and did not feel compelled to sign or comply.[4]

The Second Conference, in 1960, failed to agree on the breadth of the territorial sea or on an additional fisheries zone.

UNCLOS

The Third Conference, however, succeeded in concluding a breathtakingly comprehensive convention that is a veritable constitution of the world's seas, this time with almost all countries signing and, with the important exception of the United States, eventually ratifying it. The UN Convention on the Law of the Sea was adopted and opened for signature in Montego Bay, Jamaica, on 10 December 1982 and, later, also at the United Nations in New York. Twelve months after the deposit of the sixtieth instrument of ratification or accession, as provided for in its Article 308, the convention entered into force on 16 November 1994.

Among its many provisions, the UNCLOS prescribes methods for drawing baselines along the coasts of coastal states. In the case of an archipelagic state, the UNCLOS provides for the drawing of "straight archipelagic baselines joining the outermost points of the outermost islands and drying reefs of the archipelago". Ninety-seven per cent of the archipelagic baselines are not to exceed 100 nautical miles, while the other 3 per cent may do so up to 125 nautical miles.

From the baselines are measured the 12-mile breadth of the territorial sea, the 24-mile contiguous zone, in which the coastal state may enforce its customs, fiscal, immigration or sanitary laws and regulations, the continental shelf where the continental margin ("the sea-bed and subsoil of the shelf, the slope and the rise") extends beyond 200 nautical miles (up to 350 nautical miles), and the 200-mile exclusive economic zone, where the coastal state has the sovereign rights to explore, exploit, conserve and manage the natural resources, establish and use artificial islands and other installations, and conduct marine scientific research. The UNCLOS calls on parties with opposite or adjacent coasts to negotiate the delimitation of their overlapping EEZs — and continental shelves — or, when they fail to agree "within a reasonable period of time", resort to the dispute-settlement procedures laid down in the convention.[5]

The Philippines saw in the development and adoption of the UNCLOS a number of opportunities. One was to gain international acceptance of the archipelagic concept, which would consider archipelagos like the Philippines, Indonesia, Mauritius and Fiji as integral units, with sovereignty over the waters between their islands, rather than over collections of islands each generating its own maritime regime. Another, related objective was to obtain international recognition of the waters between the islands of the archipelago as, under certain conditions, internal. A third was to acquire the right to and responsibility for the resources within an expanse of sea up to 200 nautical miles from the baselines.

At the same time, the UNCLOS, as adopted, posed a number of challenges to the Philippines. The agreement on a 12-mile limit on the territorial sea called into question the claim that the waters between the baselines and the Treaty of Paris limits constituted part of the territorial sea. The conditions prescribed in the convention for declaring waters as internal exposed large expanses of waters between Philippine islands, such as the Sulu Sea and the Moro Gulf, to unauthorized foreign intrusion, until, under the archipelagic concept, the Philippines designated its archipelagic sealanes. The UNCLOS also heightened the ambiguity of the Philippine claim to a large part of the South China Sea, both land and water, just as it did that of the Chinese and Vietnamese claims to all of it. Finally, the Philippines has been compelled either to declare itself an archipelagic state in the full UNCLOS sense or to attribute to itself the rights but not all the obligations of such a state. (See Figures 3 and 4.)

PHILIPPINE "RESERVATIONS"

The Philippines was among the 119 countries that signed the UNCLOS on 10 December 1982, the day it was opened for signature. Despite the doubt that the convention cast on the Philippine claim on the extent of its territorial sea and other issues, the head of the Philippine delegation, Arturo Tolentino, explained upon signing the convention that his government had decided to become party to it because it established rules governing the seas and their resources, applicable to all "regardless of size or power", and thus strengthened international law. The Philippines had opposed the universal application of a specific breadth for the territorial sea, claiming an exception for itself on the grounds of history, economy and security. However, it did sign the convention, even with the universal application of the prescribed 12-mile territorial sea.

More to the point with respect to the Philippines was the fact that the convention recognized and accepted the concept of archipelago that the

Philippines had espoused together with such countries as Indonesia and Fiji. The UNCLOS recognizes the archipelagic state's sovereignty over the archipelagic waters, the air space above them, the seabed and subsoil beneath them, and the resources there, but ensures the right of foreign vessels to innocent passage through archipelagic sea lanes designated by the archipelagic state. Tolentino also explained that the UNCLOS's designation of exclusive economic zones had "lightened" the problem for the Philippines, whose 200-mile EEZ would now cover a much larger area than its "historic territorial sea", since it would extend beyond the Treaty of Paris limits except in a small corner in the northeast and cover most of the water in the area of the Spratlys that the Philippines had claimed.[6]

Upon signing the convention, the Philippines filed an "understanding", which it confirmed when it ratified the UNCLOS in May 1984. The understanding declared that the Philippines' signature on the convention would not:

* "impair or prejudice" its rights under its constitution or, as successor state to the United States, under the 1898 Treaty of Paris or the 1930 U.K.-U.S. convention;
* affect the rights and obligations of the parties under the Philippine-U.S. Mutual Defense Treaty or any other international agreement;
* "impair or prejudice" Philippine sovereignty over the Kalayaan Islands and "the waters appurtenant thereto" as well as any other territory over which the country "exercises sovereign authority".

For good measure, the Philippines stressed that its signature on the convention should not be construed as amending "pertinent" laws or presidential decrees or proclamations and affirmed its right to amend those laws, decrees and proclamations. Significantly, the understanding referred to the Philippines as an "archipelagic State". The understanding also asserted that the convention's provisions on passage through archipelagic sea lanes did not "deprive (the Philippines) of authority to enact legislation to protect its sovereignty, independence and security". It declared that the "concept of archipelagic waters is similar to the concept of internal waters under the Constitution of the Philippines", two concepts that the UNCLOS clearly distinguishes from each other.[7] Thus, the Philippines' position on whether it is an archipelagic state in the full UNCLOS sense or not was laden with ambiguity.

The Philippine "reservations" were apparently driven by the apprehension of Philippine politicians and officials about seeming to acquiesce in a diminution of Philippine "territory" or to sanction the continued violation of purported Philippine sovereignty by foreign vessels, including warships, said to be traversing waters between Philippine islands unhampered.

In any case, Article 309 of the UNCLOS states, "No reservations or exceptions may be made to this Convention unless expressly permitted by other articles of this Convention." Article 310 elaborates, "Article 309 does not preclude a State, when signing, ratifying or acceding to this Convention, from making declarations or statements, however phrased or named, with a view, *inter alia*, to the harmonization of its laws and regulations with the provisions of this Convention, *provided that such declarations or statements do not purport to exclude or to modify the legal effect of the provisions of this Convention in their application to that State* (I have provided the italics in this clause)."[8]

Singapore's Tommy Koh, from 1979 to 1982 the president of the Third United Nations Conference on the Law of the Sea, which produced the UNCLOS, stressed this point in addressing the close of the conference in December 1982. He said, "Although the Convention consists of a series of compromises, they form an integral whole. This is why the Convention does not provide for reservations. It is therefore not possible for States to pick what they like and disregard what they do not like. In international law, as in domestic law, rights and duties go hand in hand. It is therefore legally impermissible to claim rights under the Convention without being willing to assume the correlative duties."[9]

Upon its ratification of the Convention in June 1996, The Netherlands observed in its declaration, "As a general rule of international law, as stated in articles 27 and 46 of the Vienna Convention on the Law of Treaties, States may not rely on national legislation as a justification for a failure to implement the Convention." Article 27 of the Vienna Convention of May 1969 states, "A party may not invoke the provisions of its internal law as justification for its failure to perform a treaty."[10]

To be sure, other countries filed their own declarations at the time of signing or on the occasion of ratification or both. However, almost all were statements or clarifications of the countries' positions on specific provisions of the convention, on territorial or maritime disputes or claims, on the recognition of a particular signatory-state (some Arab states with respect to Israel and Greece with respect to Macedonia), or on the mode of dispute settlement.

Thus, some declarations reaffirmed countries' positions on disputed territories or made clear that being party to the convention did not imply recognition of others' territorial or maritime claims. Some insisted on prior notification or permission in the case of innocent passage, the transit of vessels that were nuclear-powered or bore nuclear materials, the conduct of military exercises, or fishing activities in the areas of the state's jurisdiction. Others would prohibit military activities in their exclusive economic zones or continental shelves, something not clearly and directly addressed in the convention. Some dealt with passage through international straits or transit to land-locked countries. Some specified using the median line in the delimitation of overlapping exclusive economic zones or continental shelves. Most declared their preferences for dispute settlement modalities; others rejected any kind of compulsory dispute settlement. Significantly, a number of states — among them Malaysia — affirmed that they were not bound by others' declarations that modified the convention's legal effect. The only country that came anywhere close to the Philippines' sweeping declaration was São Tomé and Principe, whose declaration stated, "The signing of the Convention by the Government of the Democratic Republic of São Tomé and Principe will in no way affect or prejudice the sovereign rights of the Democratic Republic of São Tomé and Principe embodied in and flowing from the Constitution of São Tomé and Principe." All other declarations affirmed the signatories' adherence to the UNCLOS and the assurance of current or future compatibility of their national laws with it.

Sure enough, several countries issued statements objecting to the Philippine declaration. The Soviet Union, its two component states that were UN members, Byelorussia (now Belarus) and Ukraine, and Soviet ally Czechoslovakia (now split into the Czech Republic and Slovakia) protested in 1985, and Australia in 1988, that the Philippines' declaration violated Articles 309 and 310 of the UNCLOS by according its domestic laws and agreements with other countries primacy over its UNCLOS obligations. Moscow, Kiev and Canberra all objected to the Philippines' consideration of archipelagic waters as internal waters.

Similarly, in an official statement, the United States insisted that, "as generally understood in international law, including that reflected in the 1982 Law of the Sea Convention, the concept of internal waters differs significantly from the concept of archipelagic waters". The statement also rejected the Philippine contention that the 1898 Treaty of Paris or the 1930 Treaty of Washington, to both of which the United States had been a party, "has conferred upon the United States, (or) upon the Republic of the Philippines as successor to the United States, greater rights in the waters surrounding the Philippine islands than are otherwise recognized in customary international law".

It is quite evident in most of these statements that the primary concern of the countries making them was the passage of their vessels through the sea lanes over which the Philippines sought to assert control. Thus, remarkably enough, the main protagonists in the then Cold War were as one in rejecting the Philippine position.

China and Vietnam deposited with the UN Secretary-General in 1985 and 1987, respectively, communications reaffirming their respective claims to the group of islands known as the Spratlys, called Nan Sha by the Chinese and Truong Sa by the Vietnamese, in response to the Philippine declaration's assertion of sovereignty over a large part of it.

DECISIONS REQUIRED

In the face of the substantial differences not only between the Philippines' official positions and those of other states but also within the country itself, the Philippines has had and, in some cases, still has to make vital policy decisions on individual issues pertaining to its maritime jurisdiction. The requirements of law enforcement and of the assertion of sovereignty, specifically in the maritime jurisdiction, demand it. The need to negotiate overlapping jurisdictions with neighbours requires it. The 13 May 2009 deadline (for the Philippines) for the notification to the UN Commission on the Limits of the Continental Shelf of the dimensions of the country's extended continental shelf gave these decisions additional urgency.

The first choice has to do with whether to consider as territorial sea the waters beyond 12 miles from the country's baselines but within the Treaty of Paris limits. If the Philippines were to continue doing so, as an apparently decreasing number of Filipinos insist upon, that would be contrary to the provisions of the UNCLOS, which provide only for a band of territorial sea to the extent of 12 miles from the baselines or coast, and no other state would recognize such an interpretation, as none does today. As others would argue and as the head of the Philippine delegation to the conference on the law of the sea seemed to do, the country's core interests could be served just as well by the UNCLOS provisions on the exclusive economic zone, which, except for a sliver of ocean northeast of Luzon, goes beyond the lines laid down by the Treaty of Paris anyway.

A related question is whether aligning the Philippines with the UNCLOS provision on the territorial sea would require an amendment to the article in the current Philippine Constitution defining the national territory. Although that article does not explicitly mention the Treaty of Paris, the term "territories over which the Philippines has sovereignty or jurisdiction" could be interpreted, as it has been, as a reference to the Treaty of Paris and other Philippine claims to sovereignty or jurisdiction. According to this interpretation, a position regarding the waters beyond the UNCLOS-prescribed 12-mile territorial sea but enclosed by the lines drawn by the treaty as anything other than part of the national territory would require a constitutional amendment, a requirement that would be all but impossible to meet in the current domestic political conditions in the Philippines.

Another question is whether the large expanses of water like the Sulu Sea and the Moro Gulf within the baselines are internal or archipelagic. The original baselines law, enacted in 1961, provided, "All waters within the baselines provided for in Section one hereof are considered inland or internal waters of the Philippines." Neither the 1968 amendment nor the 2009 law explicitly deleted this provision, although section 8 of the latter law may have done away with it. Section 8 says, "The provisions of Republic Act No. 3046 (the baselines law of 1961), as amended by Republic Act No. 5446 (of 1968), and all other laws, decrees, executive orders, rules and issuances inconsistent with this Act are hereby amended or modified accordingly." It has been pointed out that, should the Philippines insist that the bodies of water enclosed by the baselines are internal, they would be open to the unregulated intrusion of foreign vessels, since that position would not be accepted by the rest of the international community and the Philippines has little power with which to prevent such intrusions. Indeed, such vessels continue to do so with impunity. On the other hand, if they were declared as archipelagic waters, and archipelagic sea lanes were designated, they would be subject to UNCLOS rules on such sea lanes, which all parties to the convention are obliged to obey. In any case, the Philippine government seems to have settled this issue in favour of considering the waters concerned as archipelagic rather than internal. Nevertheless, there remains a dispute within the Philippines as to whether the country *must* designate archipelagic sealanes or air routes at all, since the UNCLOS merely states, in its Article 47, that an "Archipelagic State *may* designate sea lanes and air routes thereabove" (italics mine).

Article 76 of the UNCLOS allows a coastal state to declare the extension of its continental shelf if the continental margin (which "comprises the submerged prolongation of the land mass of the coastal State, and consists of the seabed and subsoil of the shelf, the slope and the rise") extends beyond 200 nautical miles but not more than 350 miles from the baselines. For this purpose, the convention created a 21-member Commission on the Limits of the Continental Shelf to receive and consider data and other material submitted by coastal states that claim continental shelves extending beyond 200 nautical miles. The Commission would then make its recommendations on the matter to the coastal state concerned and the UN Secretary-General. The UNCLOS stipulates that a coastal state seeking to establish its extended continental shelf must submit the particulars and supporting data to the Commission within ten years after the convention's entry into force for that state.[11] However, at the tenth meeting of the parties to the UNCLOS, in May 2000, a delegation raised the difficulty of some least developed countries in complying with the ten-year deadline.[12] The next meeting, in May 2001, deferred the deadline to ten years after 13 May 1999, the date of the adoption of the Commission's Scientific and Technical Guidelines, Rules of Procedure and modus operandi, for those states for which the Convention entered into force before that date. Thus, the deadline for the Philippines was 13 May 2009.[13]

It was partly in anticipation of this deadline that the Philippines redrew its baselines in March 2009. In an attempt to align the Philippine claim to a large part of the Spratlys and to Scarborough Shoal with the UNCLOS, the legislation declares a "regime of islands" for the Kalayaan islands and Scarborough Shoal. In that declaration, as discussed in Chapter 5, the law specifically invokes Article 121 of the UNCLOS. Article 121 defines an island as "a naturally formed area of land, surrounded by water, which is above water at high tide", but "(r)ocks which cannot sustain human habitation or economic life of their own shall have no exclusive economic zone or continental shelf". The March 2009 revision of the Philippines' baselines begs the question of which features that the Philippines claims in the South China Sea are islands that can sustain human habitation and thus can generate exclusive economic zones and continental shelves and which ones are mere rocks that cannot do so. Thus, the Philippines has opted for "constructive ambiguity". At the same time, the application of a "regime of islands" to the Philippines' South China Sea claims makes those claims clearer and more UNCLOS-compliant than the previous broad maritime claim that was clearly incompatible with UNCLOS rules. It also seems to apply pressure on other claimants similarly to clarify their claims.

Finally, the Philippines has to decide whether the continuing pursuit of the claim to Sabah would be worth the complications resulting from it with respect to the determination of the country's maritime jurisdiction and the world's recognition of it.

OVERLAPPING EEZS

On 11 June 1978, with the Third UN Conference on the Law of the Sea in full swing, President Ferdinand E. Marcos issued a decree under his martial-law powers establishing the Philippines' exclusive economic zone up to 200 nautical miles from the baselines. It embodies concepts previously proposed in such Latin American and Caribbean documents as the Basic Principles of the Law of the Sea in the Montevideo Declaration[14] adopted by nine countries in May 1970, the "common principles" of the Law of the Sea in the Lima Declaration[15] approved, 15–3 with one abstention, three months later, and the patrimonial-sea provisions of the Declaration of Santo Domingo[16] agreed upon by fifteen Caribbean nations, with ten affirmative votes and five abstentions, in June 1972. Most of the Marcos decree's substance found its way into the 1982 UNCLOS or reflected what were to become some of its provisions. Moreover, the decree explicitly prohibits non-Filipinos, except with the agreement of the Philippine government, from exploring or exploiting resources, carrying out research, excavation or drilling, constructing, maintaining or operating any structure or device, or doing anything contrary to the Philippines' "sovereign rights or jurisdiction" in the country's EEZ.

Like the Marcos decree with respect to the Philippines, the UNCLOS grants a coastal state an exclusive economic zone adjacent to the territorial sea with a breadth of up to 200 nautical miles from the baselines. In the zone, the coastal state has "sovereign rights" to explore, exploit, conserve and manage the natural resources, including the production of energy from the water, currents and winds. It gives the coastal state "jurisdiction" to establish and use artificial islands, installations and structures, conduct marine scientific research, and protect and preserve the marine environment. At the same time, "the coastal State shall have due regard to the rights and duties of other States". Those other states are to enjoy in the exclusive economic zone of a coastal state freedoms "of navigation and overflight and of the laying of submarine cables and pipelines, and other internationally lawful uses of the sea related to these freedoms, such as those associated with the operation of ships, aircraft and submarine cables and pipelines". They are to have "due regard to the rights and duties of the coastal State and shall comply with the laws and regulations adopted by the coastal State".

Conflicting interpretations of these "rights and duties" can lead to serious confrontations, as happened in early March 2009, when the U.S. Department of Defense charged that the USNS *Impeccable*, described as an "unarmed ocean surveillance vessel", had been "harassed" by five Chinese ships within China's EEZ, about 120 kilometers south of Hainan. Although not a party to the UNCLOS, the United States has invoked its right to freedom of navigation in the Chinese EEZ and has denied that the *Impeccable* was conducting marine scientific research, which the UNCLOS does not allow in the EEZ except with the permission of the coastal state. On the other hand, although the UNCLOS does not forbid foreign military activity in another state's EEZ, China has accused the U.S. Navy of conducting "offending activities" in China's EEZ without Beijing's permission.

The potential for conflicts to arise over activities in overlapping EEZs is even greater. Because the Philippines has a number of close neighbours across relatively narrow strips of sea, it is inevitable that its EEZ or other maritime jurisdictions should overlap with those of neighbouring countries. According to the UNCLOS, the delimitation of the maritime boundaries between countries with opposite or adjacent coasts is to be agreed upon on the basis of international law. However, until the Philippines resolves relevant fundamental issues, in terms of national territorial policy, in terms of territorial disputes with the neighbours concerned, or in terms of disputes with third countries affected, it will find it difficult, if not impossible, to reach agreement with those neighbours.

In this light, the Philippines has conducted negotiations for the delimitation of maritime boundaries with Indonesia. Involved in those negotiations, at least from the Philippine viewpoint, was the island called Las Palmas in Spanish and Miangas by the Indonesians. The island lies within the Treaty of Paris limits. However, in April 1928, Max Huber, a Swiss jurist on the roster of arbitrators of the Permanent Court of Arbitration in The Hague, ruled in favour of the Netherlands on a dispute over ownership of Las Palmas that the Netherlands and the United States had submitted for arbitration.

In the debate on the national territory in the 1934 Constitutional Convention, the chairman of the Committee on Territorial Delimitation, Nicolás Buendia, sought to insert in the definition of the national territory the phrase "as modified by the arbitral award rendered on the 4th day of April, 1928, by the Permanent Court of Arbitration at the Hague" in reference to the December 1898 and November 1900 treaties between Spain and the United States. In a letter, in Spanish, to the Committee on Style, Buendia had explained:

> The proposed Constitution approved by this august Assembly includes in the delimitation of the national territory the island of Palmas or Miangas, because this island is found within the delimitation defined in Article 3 of the Treaty of Paris of 10 December 1898, ... but after later study it has been discovered that the mentioned Palmas Island no longer belongs to the Philippine Archipelago but to Holland, by virtue of the decision rendered by the Permanent Court of Arbitration in The Hague on 4 April 1928 (translation mine)....

Buendia appended a note in English to the proposed provision on the national territory stating, "The Palmas island lies about 48 miles southwest from Cape San Agustin on the Island of Mindanao.... A few miles further off the southeast of Palmas Island are the Nanusa or Meanggis islands, which belong to the Netherlands. The island in dispute is only two miles long and three-quarters of a mile wide, has a population of about 750 persons and seems to be of practically no strategic or economic value". [17]

When Indonesia gained its independence from the Netherlands in 1945, Jakarta took over control of Miangas, which was populated by Indonesians. The protocol to the 1974 Philippines-Indonesia agreement on border trade lists Miangas among ports "in Indonesia through which barter trade can be conducted". [18]

Because of the unresolved dispute over Sabah, the Philippines-Indonesia maritime boundary delimitation talks have avoided discussion of the area westward of the point where the putative boundary between the two countries would touch upon the EEZ that Malaysia projects from Sabah. Nevertheless, Philippine officials claim that more than 90 per cent of the negotiations with Indonesia has been completed. According to Indonesian officials, they only await the results of the Philippine Supreme Court's ruling on the case filed with respect to the new baselines act and its possible impact on the 1898 Treaty of Paris.

The Philippine EEZ also overlaps with that of Palau. However, the delimitation of the maritime boundary with that neighbour to the east is low in the Philippines' priorities, probably because of the very fact that, among the maritime boundaries, the one with Palau seems to pose the least problem. There are reports, however, that Philippines-Palau delimitation talks have already begun. In any case, the overlapping EEZs between the two neighbours intersect with Indonesia's EEZ, and their definitive delimitation will have to await at least substantial progress in, if not the conclusion of, the negotiations between the Philippines and Indonesia. Those negotiations, in any case, seem to be nearing completion.

Taiwan is the Philippines' closest neighbour to the north, and an EEZ projected from it clearly overlaps with the Philippines' northern EEZ. In fact, the Philippines' EEZ encompasses much of the mainland of Taiwan. However, because of the Philippines' recognition of the People's Republic of China as the sole legal government of all of China, including Taiwan, the Philippines is unable to negotiate with the authorities in Taiwan the delimitation of the maritime boundary. Manila cannot possibly negotiate on such a politically sensitive subject as jurisdictional boundaries with a government that it does not recognise. On the other hand, negotiating with China on a boundary involving Taiwan without the latter's participation would not make much sense or have much effect. On this account, negotiations between the Philippines and Taiwan would have to wait, even if the larger issue of the conflicting claims in the South China Sea were somehow resolved. Japan's southern

EEZ, projected from the Ryukyus, also overlaps with that of the Philippines. However, it, too, overlaps with that of Taiwan. Japan also has a dispute with China over the Senkaku/Diaoyu islands.

Malaysia projects its EEZs — as well as claimed continental shelves — eastwards from the Malay peninsula and westwards from East Malaysia, that is, from Sabah and Sarawak. The EEZ that Malaysia projects from Sabah overlaps with that of the Philippines. With the Sabah issue not definitively resolved, neither Malaysia nor the Philippines has made any move to delimit any kind of maritime boundary between them, although attempts have been undertaken in the past to forge an agreement on fisheries cooperation in the disputed seas. Brunei Darussalam's claimed EEZ — and continental shelf — overlaps with those of Malaysia and the Philippines. As discussed in Chapter 5, the overlap of Brunei Darussalam's EEZ with that of Malaysia seems to have been or to be on the way to being resolved.

Notes

1. <http://www.un.org/Depts/los/convention_agreements/texts/pardo_ga1967.pdf>.
2. Raphael Perpetuo M. Lotilla, ed., *The Philippine National Territory: A collection of Related Documents* (Diliman, Quezon City: Institute of International Legal Studies, University of the Philippines Law Center, and Manila: Foreign Service Institute, Department of Foreign Affairs, 1995), p. 271.
3. Note of the Philippine Mission to the United Nations, dated 7 March 1955, in reply to the UN Secretary-General, in Lotilla, ed., *The Philippine National Territory*, p. 272.
4. <http://works.bepress.com/cgi/viewcontent.cgi?article=1071&context=david_caron>.
5. <http://www.un.org/Depts/los/convention_agreements/texts/unclos/closindx.htm>, Articles 46, 47, 48, 74 and 76.
6. Lotilla, ed., *The Philippine National Territory*, pp. 505–508.
7. <http://www.un.org/depts/los/convention_agreements/convention_declarations.htm#Philippines%20 Understanding%20made%20upon%20signature%20(10 %20December%201982)%20and%20confirmed %20upon%20ratification>:

    1. The signing of the Convention by the Government of the Republic of the Philippines shall not in any manner impair or prejudice the sovereign rights of the Republic of the Philippines under and arising from the Constitution of the Philippines.
    2. Such signing shall not in any manner affect the sovereign rights of the Republic of the Philippines as successor of the United States of America, under and arising out of the Treaty of Paris between Spain and the United States of America of 10 December 1898, and the Treaty of Washington

between the United States of America and Great Britain of 2 January 1930.

3. Such signing shall not diminish or in any manner affect the rights and obligations of the contracting parties under the Mutual Defence Treaty between the Philippines and the United States of America of 30 August 1951 and its related interpretative instruments; nor those under any other pertinent bilateral or multilateral treaty or agreement to which the Philippines is a party.

4. Such signing shall not in any manner impair or prejudice the sovereignty of the Republic of the Philippines over any territory over which it exercises sovereign authority, such as the Kalayaan Islands, and the waters appurtenant thereto.

5. The Convention shall not be construed as amending in any manner any pertinent laws and Presidential Decrees or Proclamation of the Republic of the Philippines; the Government of the Republic of the Philippines maintains and reserves the right and authority to make any amendments to such laws, decrees or proclamations pursuant to the provisions of the Philippines Constitution.

6. The provisions of the Convention on archipelagic passage through sea lanes do not nullify or impair the sovereignty of the Philippines as an archipelagic State over the sea lanes and do not deprive it of authority to enact legislation to protect its sovereignty, independence and security.

7. The concept of archipelagic waters is similar to the concept of internal waters under the Constitution of the Philippines, and removes straits connecting these waters with the economic zone or high sea from the rights of foreign vessels to transit passage for international navigation.

8. The agreement of the Republic of the Philippines to the submission for peaceful resolution, under any of the procedures provided in the Convention, of disputes under article 298 shall not be considered as a derogation of Philippines sovereignty.

8. <http://www.un.org/Depts/los/convention_agreements/texts/unclos/closindx. htm>, Article 309.

9. <http://www.un.org/Depts/los/convention_agreements/texts/koh_english. pdf>.

10. <http://untreaty.un.org/ilc/texts/instruments/english/conventions/1_1_1969. pdf>.

11. Annex II. Commission on the Limits of the Continental Shelf, United Nations Convention on the Law of the Sea <http://www.un.org/Depts/los/convention_ agreements/texts/unclos/closindx.htm>.

12. <http://daccessdds.un.org/doc/UNDOC/GEN/N00/493/29/PDF/N0049329. pdf?OpenElement>.

13. <http://daccessdds.un.org/doc/UNDOC/GEN/N01/411/52/PDF/N0141152. pdf?OpenElement>.

14. <http://www.imli.org/legal_docs/docs/A46.DOC>.
15. <http://www.imli.org/legal_docs/docs/A47.DOC>.
16. <http://www.imli.org/legal_docs/docs/A49.DOC>.
17. Lotilla, ed., *The Philippine National Territory*, pp. 206–207.
18. Ibid., p. 432.

7

WHAT NEXT?

A December 1991 "roundtable" in the Philippines recommended, among other things, "The Philippines should resolve ambiguities in Philippine law and practice towards a clear-cut, consistent and well-grounded definition of our national territory and maritime boundaries."[1] As discussed in the previous chapters, although Manila has made some significant advances in this regard, several issues pertaining to the national territory and maritime boundaries remain to be resolved.

One of these is how to treat the waters between the Philippines' archipelagic baselines and the **Treaty of Paris** limits. One view, whose adherents seem to be decreasing in number, is that the phrase in the current Constitution, "all other territories over which the Philippines has sovereignty or jurisdiction", includes all the waters within the Treaty of Paris limits, which cannot but be considered as territorial waters. This view is held, even if the quoted constitutional provision omits the explicit mention of the Spanish-American treaty or any other agreement between two foreign powers as something redolent of colonialism. A contrary view is that such an interpretation of the constitutional provision would violate the UNCLOS, which the Philippines ratified, albeit with "reservations", and which provides for territorial waters only up to 12 nautical miles beyond the baselines. A pragmatic outlook was expressed by the late Arturo Tolentino himself, a leading authority on maritime issues and the head of the Philippine delegations to all three international conferences on the law of the sea. Tolentino pointed out that, if the Philippines regarded the waters beyond the baselines merely as its exclusive economic zone, the country would have authority over the resources of a larger expanse of water than if the waters within the Treaty of

Paris limits were viewed as territorial waters, a view that would not, in any case, be shared by other states.

A related question is whether the treatment, as official policy, of the expanse of water beyond the baselines and within the Treaty of Paris limits as less than Philippine territory would require a **constitutional amendment**. This question has to be answered. A constitutional amendment would oblige Filipinos to go through a laborious and divisive political and legal process that could open many cans of worms in order to make the country's maritime regime unequivocally compliant with the UNCLOS.

A second issue is whether large bodies of water within the Philippine baselines, like **the Sulu Sea and the Moro Gulf**, can continue to be regarded as **internal waters**, when under the UNCLOS they do not qualify as such. Viewing them as archipelagic rather than as internal waters, as some suggest, would raise several questions. Would such a policy definition need a **constitutional amendment**? After all, Article 1 of the current Constitution states, "The waters around, between, and connecting the islands of the archipelago, *regardless of their breadth and dimensions* (italics mine), form part of the internal waters of the Philippines." Several pieces of legislation embody this assertion, including the 1932 fisheries act and the original, 1961 baselines law.

Would declaring itself an archipelagic state require the Philippines to designate **archipelagic sea lanes**? Some say it would be in the Philippines' national interest to do so; others argue, not necessarily. If the Philippines were to do so, where and in what directions?

The Philippines has made a "partial submission" of its **extended continental shelf**. This covers the undisputed area of Benham Rise, northeast of Luzon. When will Manila make more such submissions? What areas will they encompass?

In revising its archipelagic baselines early in 2009, the Philippines declared a **regime of islands** for Scarborough Shoal and the land features that it claims in the Spratlys. It should help if the country were to emphasise in public that this move had made the Philippine position more in line with the UNCLOS and urge China and Vietnam to do the same.

There are other issues, including the complex one of the Philippine claim to **areas of North Borneo**. How does the Philippines propose to break the deadlock on this, or should it just let the status quo persist, with its adverse impact on the Filipinos in Sabah, on the heirs of the Sultan of Sulu, and on the situation in the southernmost part of the Mindanao region?

The Philippines is particularly constrained in engaging in the bargaining and "give and take" of negotiations on jurisdictional issues. This is because certain territorial and other jurisdictional claims and restrictions are etched in the Philippine Constitution, which is extremely difficult to amend, or in laws, which can be changed only at great political peril for the proponent of change, no matter how sensible. For example, the fisheries negotiations with Malaysia bogged down in the light of the provision in the Philippine Constitution that says in its Article XII, "The State shall protect the nation's marine wealth in its archipelagic waters, territorial sea, and exclusive economic zone, and reserve its use and enjoyment exclusively to Filipino citizens."[2] This prevented the Philippine negotiators from agreeing to "joint development" in the overlapping EEZs. For a while, the boundary delimitation talks with Indonesia were stalled by the Philippine delegation's uncertainty over its authority to agree to the alienation of a piece of ocean within the Treaty of Paris limits.

Politically, Philippine leaders are loath to make policy decisions that might open them up to charges of "giving away" or "giving up" Philippine territory or otherwise putting the country at a disadvantage with respect to its neighbours. However, not resolving these issues and defining the metes and bounds of the national territory and maritime boundaries in a precise and definitive way imposes on the country and its people a number of undesirable consequences.

The Philippine Navy, Coast Guard and other law-enforcement agencies would remain unable to adopt rules of engagement that would enable them to carry out their mission of protecting the resources and otherwise upholding the law in the country's territorial waters, contiguous zone, exclusive economic zone, and continental shelves. This inability would continue to give free rein to poachers and other intruders, as it does today, to harvest resources, despoil the environment and violate Philippine sovereignty in what Manila might consider as areas where it has jurisdiction and responsibility.

Not resolving boundary issues would continue to tie the hands of Philippine negotiators in bargaining with neighbouring states on the delimitation of maritime boundaries. It would, moreover, prevent the country from entering into joint-development schemes that would be beneficial to itself and its people in areas that are disputed but where the Philippine Constitution or Philippine laws reserve "exclusively to Filipino citizens" the "use and enjoyment" of "the nation's marine wealth in its archipelagic waters, territorial sea, and exclusive economic zone".

Finally, the maintenance of the Philippine claim to parts of North Borneo remains a thorn in Philippine-Malaysian relations and hampers the operation of cooperative schemes involving Sabah, like the Brunei Darussalam-Indonesia-

Malaysia-Philippines East ASEAN Growth Area (BIMP-EAGA), which ties together all of Brunei Darussalam, eastern Indonesia, East Malaysia (Sabah and Sarawak), and Mindanao, Sulu and Palawan. It prevents the Philippines from setting up a proper consulate in Sabah from which to extend assistance to the hundreds of thousands of Filipinos there. It also withholds from the heirs of the Sultan of Sulu and/or the wider Sulu community whatever monetary compensation Malaysia offers in return for the withdrawal of the Philippine claim.

Philippine policy-makers, therefore, have to make up their collective minds, something easier said than done, on:

- The waters between the baselines and the Treaty of Paris limits;
- Whether considering those waters as other than territorial waters would require a constitutional amendment;
- How to regard the Sulu Sea and the Moro Gulf and whether doing away with their internal-waters status would require a constitutional amendment;
- Whether and where to designate archipelagic sealanes;
- Whether, when and where to make to the UN submissions on the country's extended continental shelves other than the one that it has already done;
- Whether to highlight the regime of islands declared for Scarborough Shoal and the land features of the South China Sea that the Philippines claims;
- Whether to urge publicly China and Vietnam similarly to declare regimes of islands for the land features of the South China Sea that they claim; and
- What the Philippines should do about its Sabah claim.

Notes

1.   Aileen San Pablo-Baviera, ed., *The South China Sea Disputes: Philippine Perspectives* (Manila: The Philippines-China Development Resource Center and the Philippine Association for Chinese Studies, 1992), p. 57.
2.   <http://www.chanrobles.com/article12.htm>.

INDEX

A

Abell, Anthony, 47
Abdul Kadir Mohamad, 60
Abdul Rahman, Tunku, 44, 46, 48, 50, 54
Abdullah Ahmad Badawi, 59, 80–81
Abu Hassan Omar, 57
Agoncillo, Felipe, 9
Aguinaldo, Emilio, 7
Alberto, Romulo, 96
Ali Moertopo, 51
Anderson, General, 8
Anifah Aman, 62
Aquino, Corazon C., 31, 43, 56–58, 62, 71, 85
Araneta, Salvador, 21
"archipelagic doctrine", 106
"archipelagic State", 36, 122
"archipelagic waters", 34
ARF (ASEAN Regional Forum), 89, 93, 96
Arreglado, Juan, 70–71
Aruego, Jose M., 21
ASA (Association of Southeast Asia), 51

ASEAN (Association of Southeast Asian Nations), 51, 53–56, 77, 85–89, 91–94, 96, 98, 100–101
ASEAN-China Summit, 90, 92
ASEAN Declaration on the South China Sea, 85, 87, 89
ASEAN-EU Ministerial Meeting, 89
ASEAN Ministerial Meeting, 54, 85
ASEAN Regional Forum, see ARF

B

Bacon, Robert Low, 18
B.A. Hamzah, 76
barangays, 5
Barbero, Carmelo Z., 30
baselines, of the Philippines, 29–31, 33–36, 52–53, 114
Basic Principles of the Law of the Sea in the Montevideo Declaration, 114–15
Batanes Islands, 18–19
Bateman, Sam, 76, 96–97
Bates, John C., 13
Bates Treaty, 13–16, 25
Beckman, Robert, 83

Bell, James, 50
Benny Moerdani, 51
Bernas, Joaquin, 18, 31, 55–56
Beyer, H. Otley, 41–42
BIMP-EAGA (Brunei Darussalam-
  Indonesia-Malaysia-Philippines
  East ASEAN Growth Area), 124
Bonifacio, Andrés, 6
British North Borneo Provisional
  Association, 40, 45
Brocka, Lino, 31
Brunei, claims in South China Sea,
  80–82
Buendia, Nicolás, 18–19, 116
Bundy, William P., 50

C
CAA (Commercial Arrangement
  Area), 81
Cambodian Constitution, 28
Canadian International Development
  Agency, 98
Caron, David D., 106
Carpenter Agreement, 15–16, 45, 61
Carpenter, Frank, 16, 41
Charles V, Holy Roman Emperor, 6
China
  claims in South China Sea, 74–78,
    84–88
  territorial disputes, 28–29
China National Offshore Oil
  Corporation, see CNOOC
Clinton, Hillary Rodham, 93, 96,
  100
Cloma, Tomás, 67–72, 74–75, 79
  see also "Freedomland"; Tomás
    Cloma & Associates
CNOOC (China National Offshore
  Oil Corporation), 1, 91
Cobbold Commission, 47
Cold War, 105, 112
colonial powers, 2, 27
Colony of North Borneo, 41

Commercial Arrangement Area, 81
Committee on Territorial Delimitation
  of the Constitutional
  Convention, 18
Conference on the Law of the Sea,
  106–107, 110
Conklin, Harold G., 41–42
conquistadores, 5
Constitutional Commission, 18, 23,
  31, 43, 54–55
Constitutional Convention, 26–27
Constitutional Programme of the
  Philippine Republic, 8
Constitution of 1935, 2, 18, 20–22,
  26–29, 31–33
Constitution of 1973, 2, 20, 26–29,
  31–33, 35, 55
Constitution of 1987, 2, 28, 31–33,
  37, 43, 55
Costa, Horacio de la, 12
Cuenco, Antonio V., 73
Cuenco, Mariano Jesús, 21
Cultural Revolution, 85

D
Dansalan Research Center, 13
Davis, George W., 14
Declaration on the Conduct of Parties
  in the South China Sea, see DOC
Declaration on the Territorial Sea, 77
Declaration of Santo Domingo, 115
Defensor-Santiago, Miriam, 22, 73
Deng Xiaoping, 85
Dent, Alfred, 12, 39–40, 42–43, 45,
  61
Dewey, George, 7–8
DOC (Declaration on the Conduct of
  Parties in the South China Sea),
  90, 92, 94, 100

E
ECAFE (UN Economic Commission
  for Asia and the Far East), 54

EEZ (exclusive economic zone), 1–2,
33, 83, 95, 97, 99, 107, 109, 123
overlapping, 114–18
Encarnacion, Vicente Singson, 21
Enrile, Juan Ponce, 32
ESCAP (UN Economic and Social
Commission for Asia and the
Pacific), 54
Esmail Kiram, Sultan, see Mohammad
Esmail Kiram
"exclusive fishing zone", 80

F
Federation of Malaya, 44, 47, 49
Filipinization policy, 16
Franck, Thomas, 60
"Freedom Constitution", 31
"Freedomland", 67–72, 79
see also Cloma, Tomás; Tomás
Cloma & Associates

G
García II, E. Voltaire, 18, 26–27
García, Carlos P., 67–70
Ghazali Shafie, 47–51
Gowing, Peter G., 13, 18
Granville, Earl, 40
"Greater Malaysia", 44
Guangming Daily, 68

H
Halim Ali, 59
Han Dynasty, 75
Hare-Hawes-Cutting bill, 19
Harriman, W. Averell, 50
Harrison, Francis Burton, 16, 42
Hartendorp, A.V.H., 67, 75
Hashim Djalal, 98–99
Hassan Wirajuda, 60
Hassanal Bolkiah, Sultan, 80
Home, Earl of, 44
Hontiveros, Risa, 37
Hoover, Herbert, 20

Hoyt, Ralph W., 18
Huangyan, 2
Huber, Max, 116
Humabon, Rajah, 6

I
ICJ (International Court of Justice),
46, 50, 60–61, 95
imperialism, 27
Indonesian Communist Party, 50
Indonesian Constitution, 28
Ingles, José D., 70
internal waters, 122
ISEAS (Institute of Southeast Asian
Studies), 91–92
Itu Aba island, 74, 80

J
Jabidah Massacre, 31, 51
Jamalul Alam, Sultan, 12, 39, 41, 43,
61
Jamalul Kiram, Sultan, 11
Jamalul Kiram II, Sultan, 13, 15, 58,
61, 64
heirs, 42–43
Jin Dynasty, 75
Johnson, L.M., 8
Joint Marine Seismic Undertaking, 1
jurisdiction, maritime, 19–20
jurisdiction of seabed, and Malta,105

K
Kalayaan Island Group, 1, 33, 37, 70,
72–74, 84, 95, 109, 114, 119
Katipunan ng Mga Anak ng Bayan
(Society of the Children of the
Nation), 6
Koh, Tommy, 110
konfrontasi, 49, 51

L
Laurel, José B., 32
Laurel, Salvador, 85

Legazpi, Miguel López de, 6
Lima Declaration, 115
Liwag, Juan, 30
Location Map of the South China Sea
    Islands, 76
López, Salvador P., 45, 48–49
Lotilla, Raphael Perpetuo, 32, 34
Louisiana Purchase of 1803, 29
Lu Ning, 75, 77, 82

M
Maambong, Regalado, 18
Mabini, Apolinario, 8
Macapagal-Arroyo, Gloria, 36, 73,
    90–91
Macapagal, Diosdado, 43, 45, 50
Macaskie, C.F.C., 42, 58
Mackie, J.A.C., 44
Magallona, Merlin, 37
Magellan, Ferdinand, 6
Magsaysay, Ramón, 43, 68
Mahathir Mohamad, 56, 59
Malaysia
    claims in South China Sea, 80–82
    creation of, 44–51
    see also Sabah
Malaysia Agreement, 48
"Malaysian Border Area", 50
Malaysiakini, 63
Malaysian Constitution, 28
Malolos Constitution, 9, 21, 28
Malta, and seabed jurisdiction, 105
Manglapus, Raul S., 43, 58, 85
Manila Accord, 46, 50, 61
Manila Declaration, 86, 89
MAPHILINDO (Malaysia, the
    Philippines, and Indonesia), 46,
    49, 51
Marcos, Ferdinand E., 26, 31, 50, 52,
    54–55, 59–60, 69–70, 73, 85,
    114–15
Maritime Institute of Malaysia, 76
maritime jurisdiction, 19–20

Martelino, Eduardo "Abdul Latif", 52
martial law, 26
Martial Law Regime, 71
Martínez, Carlos, 39
Mastura, Michael, 56
McDuffie, John, 20
McCulloch, boat, 7
Mexican-American War, 29
Michelmore, Laurence, 48
Mindanao, 10–18
Mindanao Plantation, 18
Ming Dynasty, 82
Mischief, Heribert, 86
Mischief Reef, 84, 86–89, 91
Mitra, Ramon, 56
Mohammad Esmail Kiram, Sultan, 43,
    53, 61
Mohammed Pulalun, Sultan, 11
Mohd Abu Bakar, 50
Montinola, Ruperto, 21
"municipal law", 33
Muslim Filipinos, 2
Muslim south, in the Philippines
    11–12
Mutual Defense Treaty, *see* Philippine-
    U.S. Mutual Defence Treaty

N
NAM (Non-Aligned Movement), 89
Nanyang Technological University, 76
National Press Club, 49
national territory, defining, 27
National University of Singapore, 83
North Borneo Company, 12, 17,
    40–41, 45

O
Oda, Shigeru, 60
Ong, Romualdo, 85
Oplan Merdeka, 52
Ople, Blas, 54
Overbeck, Gustavus Baron de, 12,
    39–40, 42–43, 45, 61

P
Pacific War, 74
Padilla, Ambrosio, 33
padjak, 12
Panglima Hassan, 15
Pardo, Arvid, 105
Peláez, Emmanuel, 45, 54
Perfecto, Gregorio, 22
Philip II, King, 6
Philippine Air Force, 86
Philippine-American War, 8, 10
Philippine Commission, 14
Philippine Constitutional Convention,
    21
Philippine declaration, 34–35
Philippine Maritime Institute, 67,
    74
Philippine National Oil Company, *see*
    PNOC
Philippine revolution, 8
Philippines, the
    Constitution of 1935, 2, 18, 20–22,
        26–29, 31–33
    Constitution of 1973, 2, 20, 26–29,
        31–33, 35, 55
    Constitution of 1987, 2, 28, 31–33,
        37, 43, 55
    baselines of, 29–31, 33–36, 52–53,
        114
    boundaries, 20
    independence, 13, 17, 26
    limits of territory, 9–10
    Muslim south, 11–12
    response to creation of Malaysia,
        44–51
    Spanish rule, 6–7
    territorial waters of, 22–23
    U.S. military expedition in, 8
Philippine-U.S. Mutual Defence
    Treaty, 35, 109, 119
PNOC (Philippine National Oil
    Company), 1, 91
Pope Alexander VI, 5

Pope Julius II, 5
Potsdam Proclamation, 67, 79
Pratt, Spencer, 7

Q
Qian Qichen, 85
Qing Dynasty, 76
Quintero, Eduardo, 27
Quirino, Elpidio, 42

R
Ramos, Fidel V., 59, 62
Ramos, Narciso, 53
Ramos-Shahani, Leticia, 57
"regime of islands", 2, 114, 122
Republic Act, 36
Romulo, Carlos P., 54, 70
Romulo, Roberto R., 58, 87
Roosevelt, Theodore, 15
Roosevelt, Franklin D., 20
Roque, Harry, 37
Royal Colonial Institute, 42

S
Sabah
    claim to, 1, 3, 27, 29–32, 37, 43,
        49–63
    see also Malaysia
Salonga, Jovito, 45, 57
San Francisco Peace Conference, 79
San Francisco Treaty, 28, 66
San Juan, Frisco, 30
Sarmiento, René, 32
Scarborough Shoal, 2, 37, 72–74,
    83–84, 95, 114, 122, 124
Schofield, Clive, 99–100
seabed jurisdiction, and Malta,105
Second World War, *see* World War II
Siazon, Domingo, 63
Sipadan and Ligitan islands, 60
Society of the Children of the Nation
    (*Katipunan ng Mga Anak ng
    Bayan*), 6

Soeharto, 51
Song Dynasty, 75
South China Sea, 3
Spain-U.S. Peace Treaty, 6–10, 30
Spanish-American War, 6–7
Spanish
    explorers, 5
    rule in the Philippines, 6–7
    sovereigns, 5
Spratly, Henry, 86
Spratly islands
    claim to, 2, 28–29, 66, 69, 72,
        74–80, 92, 95, 97, 99, 112
Storey, Ian, 99–100
Suhakam, 63
Sukarno, 46, 49–50, 59, 61
Sulu, 10–18, 40
    sultanate, 11, 39, 41, 43, 45
Sumner, Samuel, 14

T
Taft, William Howard, 14–15, 18
Tanaka, Kakuei, 67
Tang Dynasty, 75
Tang Jiaxuan, 88
Tarling, Nicholas, 44
Tatad, Francisco, 62
Thant, U, 48
Tolentino, Arturo, 10, 30, 34, 53–54,
    108–09, 121
Tomás Cloma & Associates, 70–71
    see also Cloma, Tomás;
        "Freedomland"
Tran Van Huu, 79
Treacher, W.H., 39
Treaty of Amity and Cooperation, 85
Treaty of Guadalupe Hidalgo, 29
Treaty of Paris, 9–10, 12, 18–20,
    22–24, 27, 29–30, 33, 35–36,
    71–72, 106, 109, 111–12,
    116–18, 121–24
Treaty of Peace, 6, 28, 66

Treaty of Peace and Friendship, 67
Treaty of Tordesillas, 5
Treaty of Washington, 111, 118
Turtle and Mangsee Islands, 17
Tydings-McDuffie Act, 20, 29
Tydings, Millard E., 20

U
Ulama, Ulka, 42–43
UNCLOS (United Nations
    Convention on the Law of the
    Sea), 1, 3, 19, 22–24, 30, 32–37,
    73–74, 76–78, 81, 88, 96–97,
    100–101, 107–16, 121–22
    and claims in South China Sea,
        82–84
UN Commission on the Limits of
    the Continental Shelf, 36, 83,
    112–13
UN Economic and Social Commission
    for Asia and the Pacific, see
    ESCAP
UN Economic Commission for Asia
    and the Far East, see ECAFE
United States
    acquisition of territories, 29
    involvement in the South China
        Sea, 93–94
    military expedition in the
        Philippines, 8
Universal Declaration of Human
    Rights, 68
University of British Columbia, 98
University of California, 106
University of Malaya, 50, 76
University of the Philippines, 22, 37,
    41
U.S. Asiatic Squadron, 7
U.S. Constitution, 29
USNS Impeccable, 115
USS Olympia, 7
USS Petrel, 7

V

Valencia, Mark, 97

Vargas, Pedro, 71

Vienna Convention on the Law of
    Treaties, 110

Vietnam, claims in the South China
    Sea, 78–80

Vinzons, Wenceslao Q., 21

W

Wade-Giles system, 77

Wain, Barry, 91

Wall Street Journal Asia, 91

Wang Yi, 90

Wang Yingfan, 88

Washington Convention, 17

Watherston, David, 47

Wildman, Rounsevelle, 7

Wilson, Woodrow, 16

Wong Pow Nee, 47

Wood, Leonard, 14–15

"Workshops on Managing Potential
    Conflict in the South China Sea",
    98

World War II, 66, 69, 78, 106

Wright, Luke E., 15

X

Xue Hanqin, 92

Y

Yang Jiechi, 93

Yuan Dynasty, 75

Z

Zamboanga Chamber of Commerce, 18

Zheng He, 75

Zhou Enlai, 77, 85

ABOUT THE AUTHOR

Rodolfo C. Severino is the head of the ASEAN Studies Centre at the Institute of Southeast Asian Studies in Singapore and a frequent speaker at international conferences in Asia and Europe. Having been Secretary-General of the Association of Southeast Asian Nations from 1998 to 2002, he has completed a book, entitled *Southeast Asia in Search of an ASEAN Community* and published by ISEAS, on issues facing ASEAN, including the economic, security and other challenges confronting the region. He has produced a book on ASEAN in ISEAS' Southeast Asia Background Series and one on the ASEAN Regional Forum. His views on ASEAN and Southeast Asia have also been published in *ASEAN Today and Tomorrow*, a compilation of his speeches and other statements. He has co-edited two books: *Whither the Philippines in the 21*[st] *Century?* and *Southeast Asia in a New Era*, which is intended for pre-university students. He writes articles for journals and for the press. Before assuming the position of ASEAN Secretary-General, Severino was Undersecretary of Foreign Affairs of the Philippines, the culmination of thirty-two years in the Philippine Foreign Service. He twice served as ASEAN Senior Official for the Philippines and is one of the Philippines' Experts and Eminent Persons for the ASEAN Regional Forum. Severino has a Bachelor of Arts degree in the humanities from the Ateneo de Manila and a Master of Arts degree in international relations from the Johns Hopkins University School of Advanced International Studies. He is a member of the Advisory Board of *The Fletcher Forum of World Affairs*, the journal of the Fletcher School of Tufts University.

Figure 1. The Philippines within the Treaty of Paris limits and the U.S.-U.K. Maritime Boundary

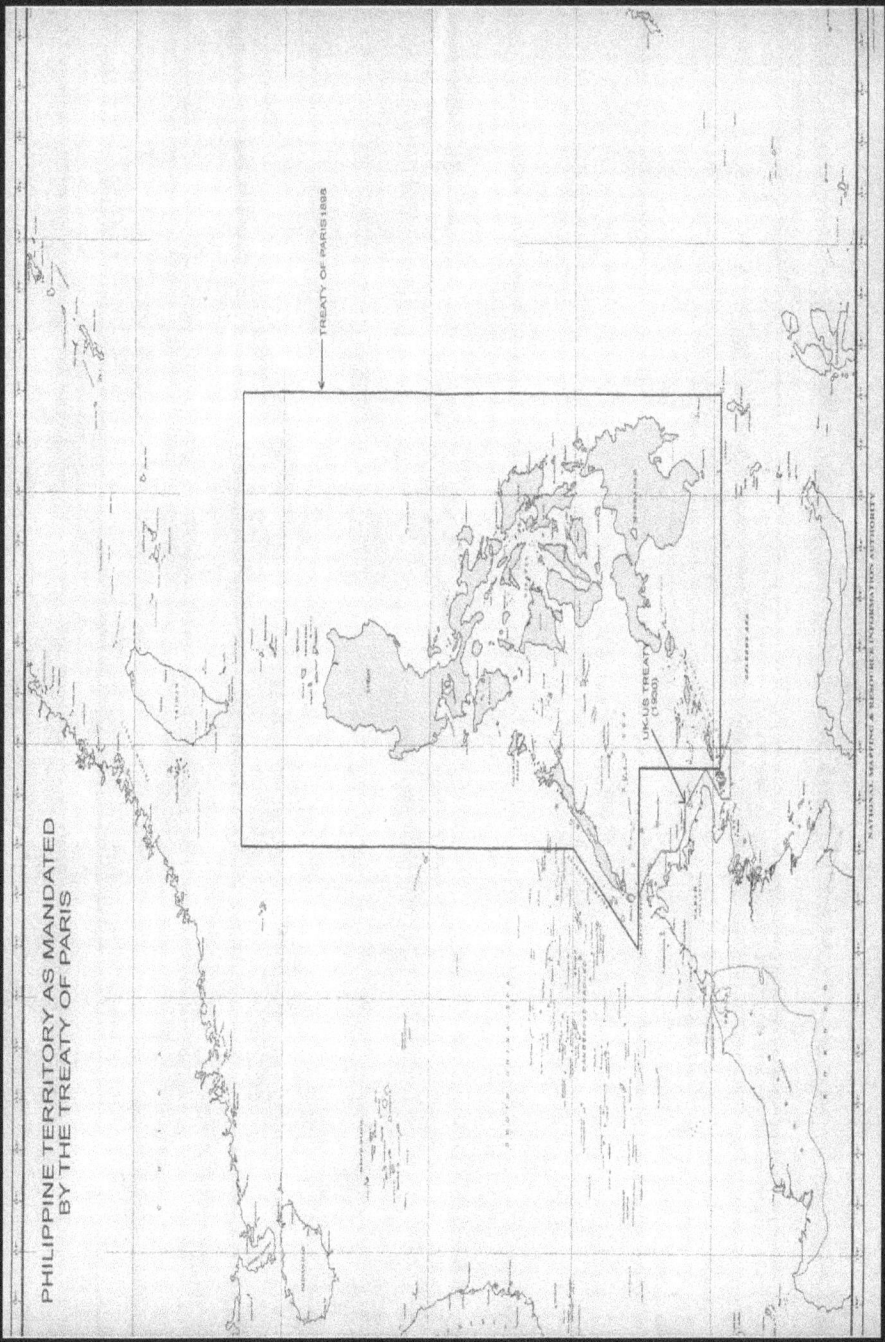

PHILIPPINE TERRITORY AS MANDATED
BY THE TREATY OF PARIS

TREATY OF PARIS 1898

UK-US TREATY
(1930)

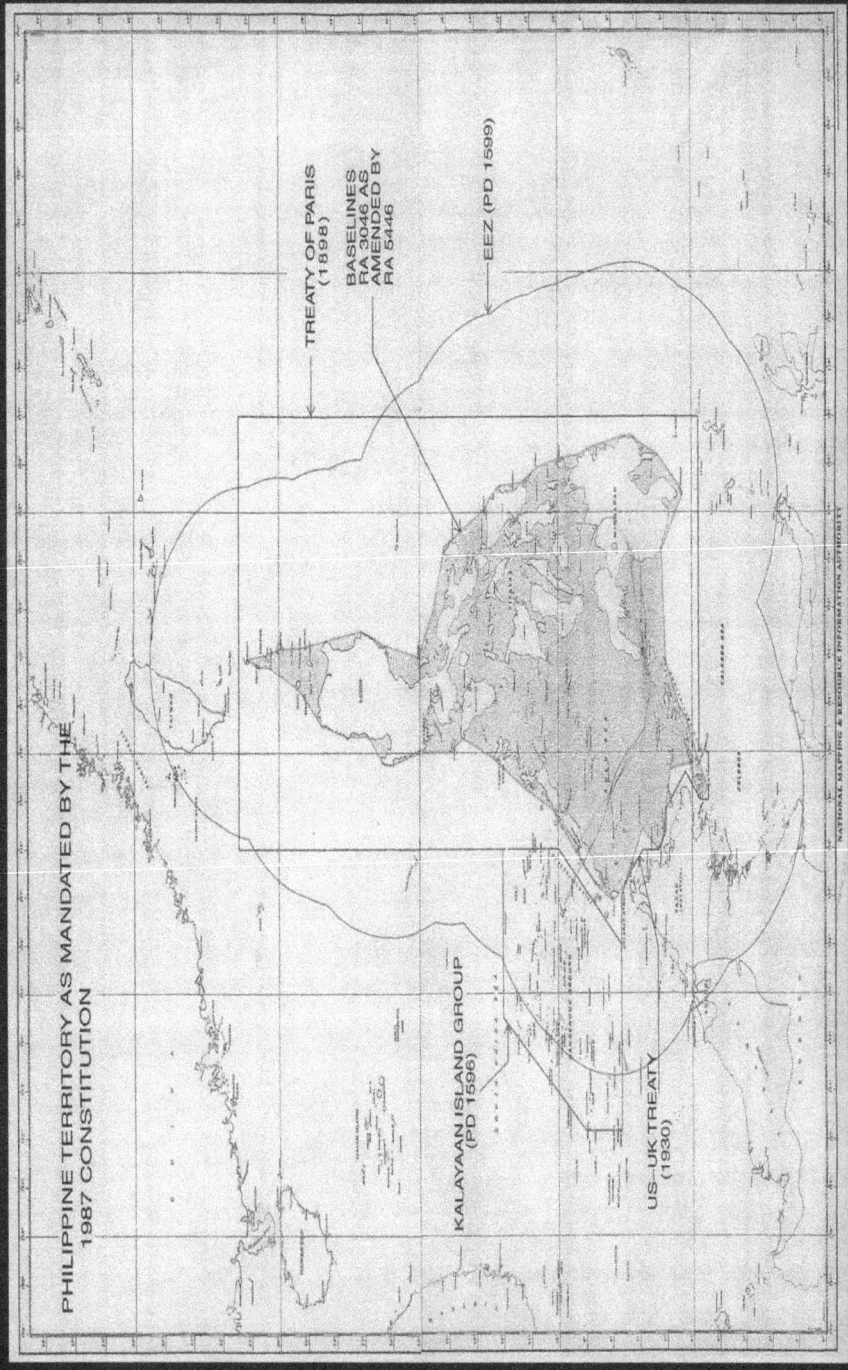

Figure 2. The Philippine national territory and maritime claims as defined by the 1987 Constitution, the 1968 Baselines Act, the 1978 Presidential Decree establishing the Philippines' exclusive economic zone, and the 1978 Presidential Decree laying claim to the Kalayaan Island Group

Maritime Zones under UNCLOS

LEGEND

Baselines

Archipelagic and internal waters (572,307 Km²)

Territorial Sea (12 M) (117,646 Km²)

Contiguous Zone (24 M) (121,830 Km²)

EEZ (200 M) (1,178,378 Km²)

Juridical Continental Shelf (200 M) (1,178,378 Km²)

Total water area (= 1,990,161 Km²)

vs

Total land area (= 299,088 Km²)

Sovereign power to enforce laws

Sovereign rights to exploit resources

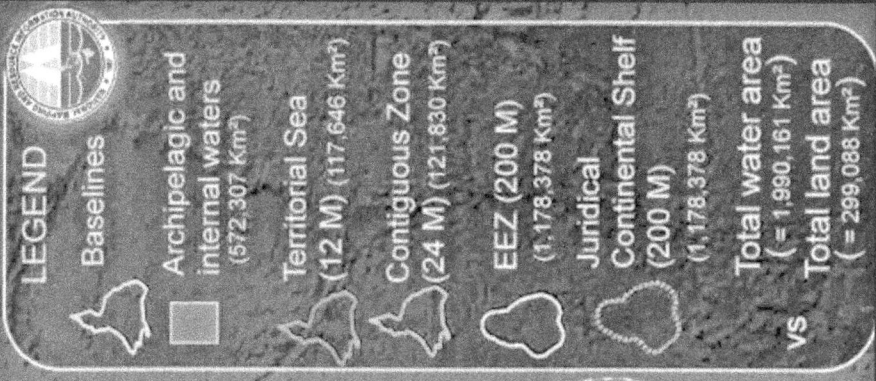

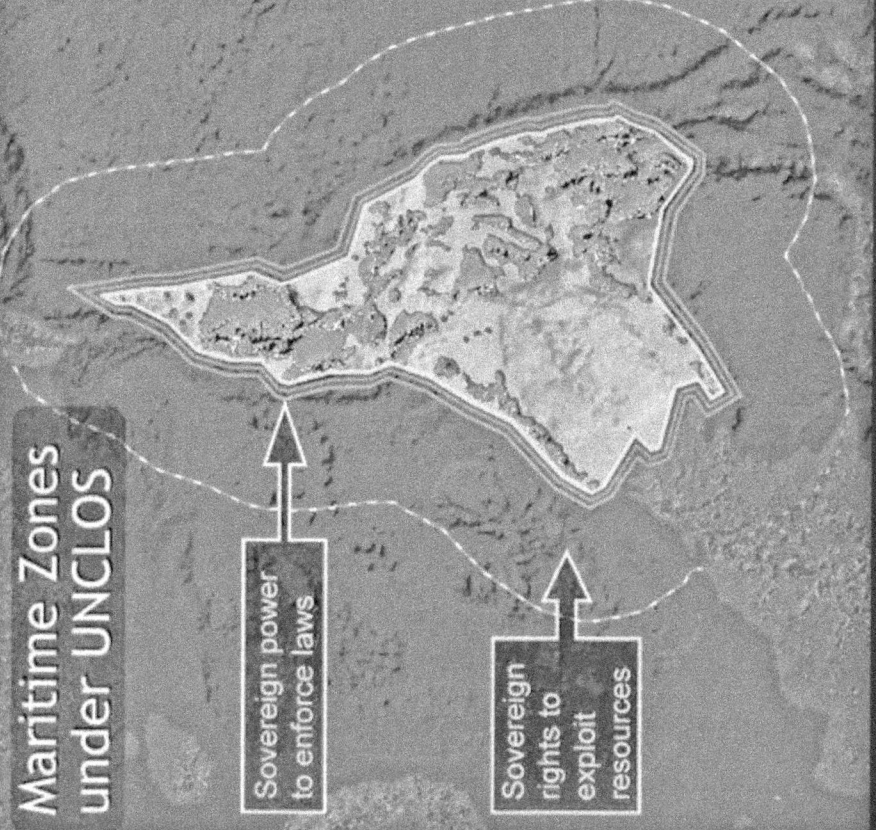

Source: Reproduced with permission of Professor Rommel C. Banlaoi, Chairman of the Board and Executive Director, Philippine Institute for Peace, Violence and Terrorism Research.

Figure 4. Philippine Territory Taking into Consideration the Provisions of UNCLOS

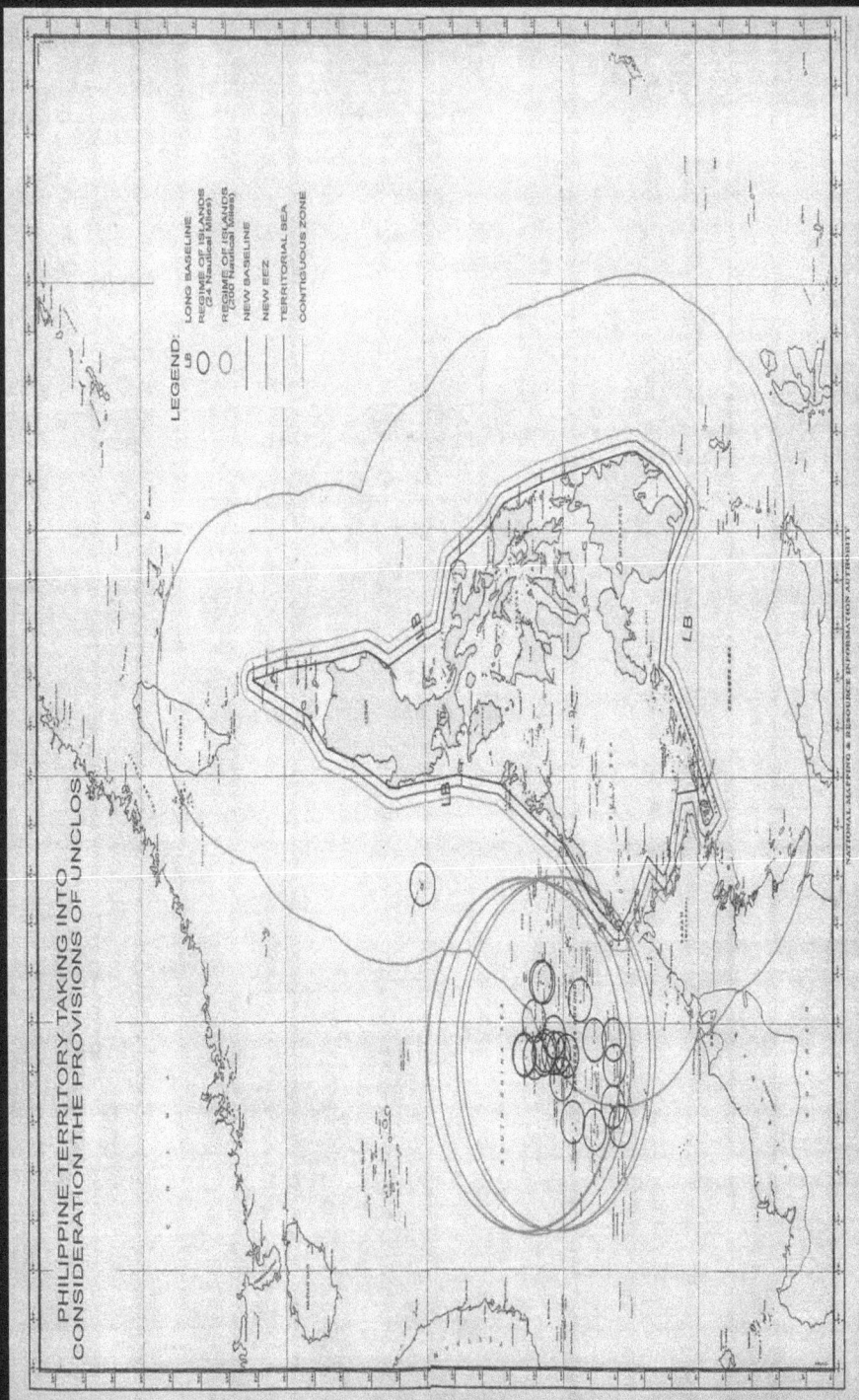

PHILIPPINE TERRITORY TAKING INTO
CONSIDERATION THE PROVISIONS OF UNCLOS

LEGEND:
LB   LONG BASELINE
○   REGIME OF ISLANDS
            (24 Nautical Miles)
○   REGIME OF ISLANDS EEZ
            (200 Nautical Miles)
            NEW BASELINE
            NEW EEZ
            TERRITORIAL SEA
            CONTIGUOUS ZONE

NATIONAL MAPPING & RESOURCE INFORMATION AUTHORITY